NEW ZEALAND

NATURE HEROES

The head of Tennyson Inlet, Marlborough Sounds.

NEW ZEALAND NATURE HEROES

GILLIAN CANDLER

pb potton & burton

CONTENTS

INTRODUCING
NEW ZEALAND NATURE HEROES

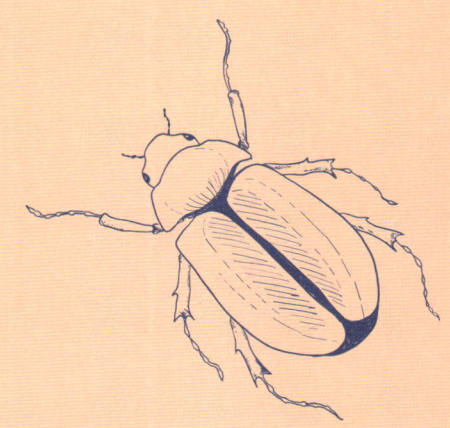

Ever wondered how people get to be heroes? Or how you, too, could be a hero? New Zealand's natural world is in real need of heroes, with birds, lizards, insects and marine creatures under serious threat from introduced predators, loss of habitat and pollution. The good news is there are many people working hard to save our unique animals and plants and the wild places where they live. These heroes have taken up the challenge to be guardians, to be kaitiaki of the natural world, and they are the subject of this book.

There are so many nature heroes to choose from in New Zealand. In fact, the more I looked, the more I found. There are people who have saved forests, set up wildlife rescue centres, planted thousands of trees, protected kiwi, discovered unusual lizards, and many more. I wish I could have included them all.

The nature heroes in this book come from all walks of life. Some lived in the past, while, of those alive today, some are volunteers, others are trained scientists, some are young, some not so young. The one thing they all have in common is their passion for the natural world.

Each of the personal stories also has information about a featured animal, plant or habitat, such as the royal albatross that Lance Richdale worked so hard to save. Others include what scientists want us to learn more about, such as the rocky shore Betty Batham spent her life studying. One story features some conservation dogs, which are trained to help save wildlife; another is about epiphytes that grow in trees. When I met Pātaka Moore and Caleb Royal, they suggested that the Mangapouri Stream they are working to restore should actually be the hero.

Although some of the nature heroes in this book worked alone, most of them would say they couldn't have done their work without help from others. For example, in saving the tīeke/saddleback, Don Merton worked with school children gathering data on tīeke, botanists identifying tīeke habitat, sound engineers recording tīeke calls and other bird experts.

Many of the nature heroes have also written books, created websites or started up campaigns for their projects, such as Richard Henry's book *The Habits of the Flightless Birds of New Zealand* in 1903, Catherine Kirby's 'Tree Project' exhibition and Riley Hathaway's Young Ocean Explorers videos and website. This is because an important part of being a nature hero is helping others become aware of New Zealand's wildlife and wild places and understanding what needs to be done to protect or save them.

Top: A cicada on a summer's day.
Above: A pōhutukawa in full flower.
Opposite, top: South Island robin.
Opposite, below: Harakeke/flax flowers.

TAKING ACTION

This book is packed with activities and ideas for ways you can take some action to save your local wildlife and contribute to the work of scientists.

While you might not be able to find a new species of wētā, as George Gibbs did, or take care of rescued lizards like Nicola Toki, there are many things you can do to make the survival of these species more certain and maybe become a nature hero yourself.

Up-to-date information can be found on the website that accompanies this book: www.discovernature.nz/nature-heroes

KEEPING SAFE

Before you start any project, think carefully about how you (and your team) can keep safe. Here are some tips:

- ☆ make sure you can use all equipment safely
- ☆ ask adults for assistance when you need it
- ☆ know the water safety code
- ☆ Adventure Smart has advice on how to keep safe on land and water: www.adventuresmart.nz

There are helpful resources and further information on pages 72–75

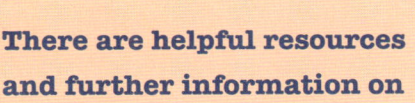

RICHARD HENRY

THE GRANDFATHER OF CONSERVATION

In the late 1800s, while he was working in the bush around Te Ānau, Richard Henry spent a lot of time observing the behaviour of native birds and other animals. He began to realise that flightless birds such as the kākāpō and kiwi might soon become extinct, as they were an easy meal for the rats, ferrets, stoats and weasels that had been introduced and were spreading throughout New Zealand. Rats had arrived, unwanted, from ships, but ferrets, stoats and weasels had been deliberately released by farmers to kill the rabbits (which were also introduced into New Zealand by well-meaning people). These animals had become a plague and were devastating farms.

It was difficult for conservationists to persuade the government to set up sanctuaries, but eventually the government agreed, and three sanctuaries were created: Hauturu (Little Barrier Island) in the Hauraki Gulf, Kāpiti Island, north of Wellington, and Tau Moana (Resolution Island) in Fiordland's remote Dusky Sound.

Richard Henry was asked to be caretaker of Resolution Island in 1894. Like many people who lived in Fiordland 120 years ago, Richard Henry was an adventurer who had learnt lots of practical skills. He knew how to camp, cook, grow food, hunt, build wooden houses, build and sail boats, train dogs and track wildlife.

At first, he and his young assistant captured kākāpō and kiwi and transferred them to the island by boat. His dog, which was probably the first conservation dog in New Zealand, wore a muzzle so it did not harm the birds it found, and it wore a bell so Richard Henry could keep track of it.

Sadly, Resolution Island wasn't as safe as he and others thought. Poachers, sealers and hunters brought or threatened to bring dogs to the island. But worst of all, stoats and weasels were able to swim across from the mainland. When he discovered this, Richard Henry tried to trap these predators, but more kept arriving. In 1908, disheartened after years of work, he gave up and moved to be caretaker of Kāpiti Island.

It must have been extremely sad for Richard Henry to have to abandon his work at Resolution Island. If only he could be alive today to visit Anchor Island, which lies just off Resolution Island in Dusky Sound. Now cleared of pests, it is a crucial kākāpō sanctuary, where the birds are successfully breeding.

TIMELINE OF
RICHARD HENRY

1845: Born in Ireland.

1851: Immigrated by ship with his family to Australia. He was six years old.

1874: Travelled by ship to live in New Zealand. Here, he took on many different jobs from boat building to controlling rabbits.

1883: Settled down to live by Lake Te Ānau.

1894: Became caretaker of Resolution Island.

1903: Wrote *The Habits of Flightless Birds of New Zealand: with notes on other New Zealand birds*.

1908: Moved to be ranger on Kāpiti Island.

1912: Retired to the mainland.

1929: Died aged 84.

Clockwise from top left: Richard Henry by his boatshed on Pigeon Island; the beach below his house on Pigeon Island; a captive kiwi; his dog Lassie, muzzled and ready for work; a map of Resolution Island, Pigeon Island and Dusky Sound, Fiordland.

'Kakapo is from two Maori words: kaka, a parrot, and po, night – which is very becoming, because I think they are the only parrots that feed at night.'

RICHARD HENRY

CARING FOR KĀKĀPŌ

Richard Henry observed all the birds around him in the forest of Fiordland, including weka, kiwi, penguins and kākāpō. He wrote down his observations and in 1903 published them in a book called *The Habits of Flightless Birds of New Zealand: with notes on other New Zealand birds*.

Richard Henry observed that kākāpō males scratch out a dust bowl and create a well-worn track, usually on a ridge. The male tries to attract females to this area with his booming calls. It took 70 years for scientists to confirm Henry's observations were correct. Scientists now call this a 'track and bowl' system but Richard Henry described it as a 'bower'. He wrote:

'I think it likely that the males take up their places in these "bowers", distend their air-sacks and start their enchanting love songs; and that the females love the music and parade and come up to see the show.'

Henry also tried to figure out why chicks weren't born every year. Now scientists know that kākāpō breed in a 'mast year', when rimu (or other fruit) is plentiful. But back then, Richard Henry joked that all the kākāpō must get together for a meeting to decide whether to breed or not!

Kākāpō are flightless, have a strong musky smell, and are quite tame and curious, so they easily fall prey to introduced mammals that hunt by scent.

After Richard Henry's efforts failed, not much more was done to save kākāpō until the Kākāpō Recovery programme was set up. From the 1970s, kākāpō were taken from Fiordland and Stewart Island to islands such as Whenua Hou (also called Codfish Island) off Stewart Island/Rakiura, where they could be safe from predators. Only 51 birds were known to be alive in 1995, but scientists have worked hard to increase the population, giving the chicks the best possible chance to survive. Now there are nearly 160 birds.

STRONG SWIMMERS

Stoats have been found on islands more than 2 kilometres from the mainland. They have also shown they are able to swim long distances. Resolution Island was easily reached as it is less than 1 kilometre from the mainland. Now, all island sanctuaries have traps set around the coast, and if the island is close to the mainland, there must be traps on the mainland coast as well.

Top left: A kākāpō on Whenua Hou, an island sanctuary off Stewart Island/Rakiura. Top: The stoat, a deceptively friendly looking predator. Above: Baiting a predator trap with a hen's egg, to catch stoats. Opposite top: Changing a kākāpō's transmitter on the Anchor Island sanctuary, Fiordland. Opposite below: The view into Dusky Sound from the Anchor Island sanctuary, Fiordland.

Kakāpō facts

* flightless but can climb
* vegetarians
* only breed when there is a lot of food around
* adults weigh 1-4 kg!
* females look after chicks

ISLANDS CAN GET TOO FULL

As bird populations increase on island sanctuaries, there may be not enough food or suitable habitats for all the animals. One solution is to build sanctuaries on the mainland, protected by predator-proof fences. All sanctuaries, even the islands, need to keep a watch out for rats and other predators, so you will see traps set along the coast of an island or near a sanctuary's surrounding fence.

TAKING ACTION: TRACKING & TRAPPING PESTS

Conservation is about saving native wildlife, so it might seem strange that we have to kill other animals to achieve this. Unfortunately, introduced animals such as stoats, weasels, rats, hedgehogs and even mice can wipe out entire native species. To protect native animals, these introduced animals must be killed, as sending them back to where they came from isn't an option.

Trapping technology has improved a lot since Richard Henry tried to lure stoats and weasels into a box propped up on a stick. Now we use more effective traps that kill as quickly and humanely as possible. Some traps can even reset themselves.

You can help make your garden into a sanctuary for the birds and lizards that live there. Or you might like to work together with others to protect wildlife in your local park or your school grounds.

Above: A chew card installed on the trunk of a tree and a tracking tunnel waiting for a visitor. Below: The evidence left behind by two kinds of visitors. Can you work out that a stoat and mice walked over the sponge?

~~~

ACTIVITY

MAKING A TRACKING TUNNEL & CHEW CARDS

To find out what pests live in your backyard, you can build a tracking tunnel to see what animals' footprints are left behind. You can also create chew cards that the pests will bite. You will need to be a pest detective to identify the footprints and bite marks to find out what animal has been there. A helpful website is www.pestdetective.org.nz.

TRACKING TUNNEL

You will need:

- ☆ empty plastic milk bottles or cartons
- ☆ craft knife
- ☆ black plastic or paper and tape
- ☆ food colouring, sponge, tray
- ☆ white paper
- ☆ peanut butter or other bait

METHOD

1. Cut the ends off a milk bottle or carton so it forms a tunnel; put two or more together to make a longer tunnel.
2. Darken the tunnel by wrapping it in black plastic or black paper.
3. Place white paper in the tunnel. Wet the sponge with food colouring and place in a tray in the tunnel, with a small quantity of peanut butter or other lure in the middle of the sponge.

4. Leave it outside on a dry night to see what animals visit your tunnel. Do this for several nights with a fresh piece of paper each night. (Make sure your tunnel can't tip over – you may need to put a stone on top to keep it steady.)
5. Use the Pest Detective guide, www.pestdetective.org.nz, to identify by their footprints which animals visited your tunnel.

CHEW CARDS

You will need:

- ☆ **corrugated plastic, e.g. Corflute or used plastic, such as 'For Sale' signs or election placards**
- ☆ **nails**
- ☆ **peanut butter or other bait**
- ☆ **scissors or Stanley knife**

METHOD

1. Cut the plastic into small rectangles 10 cm by 20 cm and fold each in half.
2. Smear peanut butter on the plastic and poke some into the hollow part of the plastic using a nail.
3. Nail or attach the chew cards to trees or fence posts where you think hedgehogs, rats or mice might be; near a compost bin is a good place.
4. Leave out for a week and then look for bite marks. Match these to pests using photos online and use www.pestdetective.org.nz

NEXT STEPS

Once you have worked out what pests are in your garden, it's time to set some traps. You can contact your local pest-free or predator-free group for suitable traps, or buy rat and mouse traps from a hardware store. Traps should be put inside tunnels to keep small children, birds and pets safe. If you have carpentry skills, you can make a tunnel yourself; see Resources and Further Information (page 72) for where to find instructions.

WANT TO DO MORE?

Find out about the Kākāpō Recovery programme and what you can do to help or join a local sanctuary project. You could also learn how to identify pest droppings, as well as other tracks and signs when walking in the bush.

TIP

Remember: some of the animals walking through your tracking tunnel might not be pests. For example, you might find the footprints of wētā or lizards.

rabbit

ship rat

possum

norway rat

stoat

mouse

hedgehog

These paw prints might help you work out who has visited your tracking tunnel. (They are reproduced at about half their actual size with each square representing 1 cm².) Remember that actual tracks will look messier, there will often be parts of the print missing, and rats especially, tend to leave more of a scratchy trail rather than clear prints. See example on page 12.

PÉRRINE MONCRIEFF

BIRD & PARKS CAMPAIGNER

Pérrine Moncrieff was always very interested in nature, and birds in particular. She was born in England and when she, her husband and their sons travelled to New Zealand in 1921, they were so delighted with the country and the wildlife they decided to stay, settling in Nelson.

As she couldn't find a good field book on New Zealand birds, Pérrine Moncrieff set about writing one. She had the help of several scientists, and she received permission to use information about introduced birds from a similar publication in Britain. *New Zealand Birds and How to Identify Them* was so popular, it was still available in a revised fifth edition 35 years after it was first published in 1925. Moncrieff dedicated the book 'to the children of New Zealand'.

In the 1920s and 1930s, native birds were not as well protected as they are now. Fishermen shot native black shags to protect introduced fish such as trout. Hunters regularly shot godwits and other migrating birds. Ornithologists (scientists who study birds) also killed birds for museum collections. Some ornithologists did what seems like very cruel experiments, for example, seeing how long a chick would last without its parents. Pérrine Moncrieff was shocked by this behaviour and she worked hard to protect birds.

She influenced many people through her involvement in the Native Bird Protection Society (later renamed the Royal Forest and Bird Protection Society, and now known as Forest & Bird). She and her husband donated land they owned to create reserves for wildlife. She also fought to protect bird habitats at Lake Rotoroa, in what is now Nelson Lakes National Park, where black shags were being killed, and Farewell Spit in Golden Bay, where godwits were being killed.

Pérrine Moncrieff was very good at using publicity and she was always busy writing for newspapers and holding meetings trying to encourage people to save forests and wild places. Her biggest success was a seven-year campaign to create Abel Tasman National Park, which was opened in 1942. She then served on the park board for over 30 years and also became an honorary ranger.

'The importance of my mission is to save the wonderful forest and birds of New Zealand'

PÉRRINE MONCRIEFF

Pérrine Moncrieff's bestselling book sold many thousands of copies over a 35-year period.

Above: Coquille Bay in Abel Tasman National Park.
Right: A Girl Guide from 1925, wearing the black stockings that Pérrine Moncrieff objected to.

NATURE DIARY COMPETITION

For 30 years, Pérrine Moncrieff organised an annual Nature Diary competition for school children in Nelson. Children were encouraged to keep a daily diary throughout October. Entries ranged from observations of a fantail nest to collections of leaves. She would then summarise the best entries in an article in the *Nelson Evening Mail*.

GIRL GUIDE LEADER

In 1924 Pérrine Moncrieff became the first Girl Guide commissioner in Nelson. She worked hard to publicise the guide movement and recruit girls to join, believing Girl Guides provided a good opportunity for young women to get out into nature and learn outdoor and other life skills. Moncrieff wanted the girls to wear practical clothes and was against them having to wear black stockings while hiking. When she realised she couldn't change the uniform rules, she resigned.

BIRD OBSERVATION

In *New Zealand Birds and How to Identify Them*, Pérrine Moncrieff explained that anyone could contribute to the store of knowledge about birds. This is perhaps even more true today than in 1925 when she wrote it. Now, bird watchers (adults and children) can use online tools or Apps such as Nature Watch NZ and e-Bird to share what they have seen and seek help with bird identification. They can also connect to scientists through citizen science projects such as a Bioblitz.

Pérrine Moncrieff's tips for getting to know different species are still just as relevant today. She pointed out how we recognise people from a distance not just from their clothes and shape but also from the way they walk, and from other movements such as their hand gestures. In the same way, bird species can be recognised if you get to know the way they move, their habitat and their colours.

Recognising and identifying birds around your house or school is a good way to start. Get to know the sizes of a few common birds. Then, when you see a bird you don't recognise, ask yourself is it larger or smaller than the ones you know?

Here are some examples:

- ☆ pīwakawaka/ fantail, 16 centimetres
- ☆ sparrow, 15 centimetres
- ☆ blackbird, 25 centimetres
- ☆ tūī, 30 centimetres
- ☆ kererū, l50 centimetres

In her spare time Pérrine Moncrieff painted watercolours. This one is of pīwakawaka/ fantails in Abel Tasman National Park.

Other things to notice: how different each of their beaks and feet are; how they stand or fly; where they like to spend their time.

As birds often stay quite still, Pérrine Moncrieff suggested children (and adults) learn to train themselves to see details. To do this, concentrate on a particular spot and pay attention to all the detail you see in that spot, for example, you might notice that although the tree looks green, in that particular place you can see a reddish leaf, or there is a tiny flower or a bent twig. Then focus somewhere else and look at the details there. This trains your eye.

You can do the same to train your hearing: watch and/or listen to a tūī sing and try to catch all the sounds it makes. Close your eyes and listen to the sounds in your neighbourhood, then open them and see if you can work out where the noises are coming from.

QUIET & RESPECTFUL

'No bird observation or photography should be carried out at the expense of the bird,' said Pérrine Moncrieff, who was concerned that bird-watching might disturb birds or cause them harm. She said observers should be so quiet and careful that the bird wouldn't even realise it is being watched.

PERRINE MONCRIEFF'S BIRD OBSERVATION EQUIPMENT LIST:

- patience, sharp eyes and keen ears
- binoculars
- notebook and pencil
- something to sit on
- camera

Pérrine Moncrieff signing her new book in 1976, with Nelson bookseller Jill Blechynden.

BEING A CITIZEN SCIENTIST

'Citizen science' is the term used to describe how people who aren't trained as scientists can still contribute to scientific knowledge. For example, bird photographers often catch important details in their pictures that can be useful. From photos of shining cuckoos (pīpīwharauroa), scientists have been able to identify what food these cuckoos eat because many photos showed shining cuckoos with caterpillars in their beaks. It seems they are able to eat caterpillars that would be poisonous to other birds.
See nzbirdsonline.org.nz.

TAKING ACTION: COUNTING BIRDS

Once you can identify a few different species of birds you can add to our knowledge of New Zealand birds by taking part in a bird count. A bird count can tell us whether a species is declining or at risk of extinction. It can also tell us whether actions such as planting trees or trapping pests are making a difference to bird populations.

Some of the problems you may encounter when you are counting birds might be birds flying somewhere else and being counted twice, birds hiding in the bush not being counted at all, or seeing so many birds it's hard to count them.

Scientists know it is impossible to count every single bird. But if we use the same method each time we do a count, we can compare the results and make a note of what the differences are. Also, the more people who take part, the more accurate the data will be.

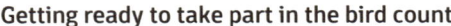

TAKING PART IN A BIRD COUNT

Because birdlife is an important part of the environment, every year at the end of June, people all across New Zealand count the birds that live in their gardens, parks and school grounds as part of the New Zealand Garden Bird Survey. Scientists share what they find out with the public on the Landcare Research website (see Resources page 72). You can also find previous survey results there.

Getting ready to take part in the bird count

Go outside and see if you know the names of all the birds you see in your garden or street. Look up the birds you don't know on the Garden Bird Survey website or NZ Birds Online. Use Pérrine Moncrieff's tips to learn more about the different birds in your garden. Keep doing this until you are familiar with the birds you see most days. There are also some quizzes and other resources on the website that you can use to improve your knowledge.

Do a practice run of the Garden Bird Survey

- ☆ Write down a list the names of birds you normally see, so all you will need to do on the day of the survey is record the numbers of birds seen.
- ☆ Find somewhere to sit where you can get a good view (this could be inside looking out).
- ☆ Look and listen for birds for half an hour.
- ☆ When you see birds, write down the number you see next to the species name.
- ☆ If you see a bird that's not on your list, add it on.
- ☆ Were there any birds you had problems recognising? Did anything go wrong with the survey? Keep practising until you recognise all the birds and can count large numbers of birds quickly (if there are large numbers).

Take part in the Garden Bird Survey

- ☆ Choose one day that suits you within the survey week.
- ☆ Prepare your list or print out the tally sheet from the website.
- ☆ Look and listen for birds for an hour.
- ☆ When you see birds, put the number seen next to the species name.
- ☆ At the end of the hour look at your results. Circle the largest number of each bird seen at any one time.
- ☆ Fill in the survey form online.

TIP

The Great Kererū Count is usually held in September. It is an easy bird count to take part in because the only bird you have to be able to identify is the kererū/New Zealand pigeon.

TIP

You can use the e-Bird App or website all year round to record the birds you see. Observations entered into e-Bird between now and 2024 can contribute to the New Zealand Bird Atlas, which maps where different species of birds live and their numbers. See www.birdatlas.co.nz for more information.

TALLY SHEET

New Zealand GARDEN BIRD SURVEY

Manaaki Whenua
Landcare Research

WHAT TO DO

1. Select a garden, park or school.
2. Choose any ONE day.
3. Look for birds for ONE hour.
4. **Use this tally sheet** to record for each species the HIGHEST number seen (or heard) at one time.

EXAMPLE:

If you see 2 blackbirds at the same time, cross 2.

⊠⊠ 3 4 5 6 7

If you then see 4 blackbirds together, cross up to box 4, not 6.

⊠⊠⊠⊠ 5 6 7

If you later see 3 blackbirds, stay at 4. Do not add up to 7.

⊠⊠⊠⊠ 5 6 7

If the count exceeds the boxes, then enter the final number into the space provided by the bird's name.

5. Submit your results online at:
gardenbirdsurvey.landcareresearch.co.nz

Please don't send us this sheet

Male ♂
Female ♀

| Small birds 15cm or less | Medium-sized birds Up to 30cm | Large birds Over 30cm |

Bellbird _____

| 1 2 3 4 5 6 |
| 7 8 9 10 11 12 |
| 13 14 15 16 17 18 |
| 19 20 21 22 23 24 |

Blackbird _____

| 1 2 3 4 5 6 |
| 7 8 9 10 11 12 |
| 13 14 15 16 17 18 |
| 19 20 21 22 23 24 |

Chaffinch _____

| 1 2 3 4 5 6 |
| 7 8 9 10 11 12 |
| 13 14 15 16 17 18 |
| 19 20 21 22 23 24 |

Dunnock _____

| 1 2 3 4 5 6 |
| 7 8 9 10 11 12 |
| 13 14 15 16 17 18 |
| 19 20 21 22 23 24 |

Fantail _____

| 1 2 3 4 5 6 |
| 7 8 9 10 11 12 |
| 13 14 15 16 17 18 |
| 19 20 21 22 23 24 |

Goldfinch _____

| 1 2 3 4 5 6 |
| 7 8 9 10 11 12 |
| 13 14 15 16 17 18 |
| 19 20 21 22 23 24 |

Greenfinch _____

| 1 2 3 4 5 6 |
| 7 8 9 10 11 12 |
| 13 14 15 16 17 18 |
| 19 20 21 22 23 24 |

Gull - black-backed _____

| 1 2 3 4 5 6 |
| 7 8 9 10 11 12 |
| 13 14 15 16 17 18 |
| 19 20 21 22 23 24 |

Gull - red-billed _____

| 1 2 3 4 5 6 |
| 7 8 9 10 11 12 |
| 13 14 15 16 17 18 |
| 19 20 21 22 23 24 |

Magpie _____

| 1 2 3 4 5 6 |
| 7 8 9 10 11 12 |
| 13 14 15 16 17 18 |
| 19 20 21 22 23 24 |

Continued overleaf

Photographs by: Andrew Walmsley, Tom Marshall, Craig MacRaerie, Brian Matera, Roger Smith. Anna Ayrad. www.istock.com

Above: The tally sheet that is used in the New Zealand Garden Bird Survey. You can download these from www.landcareresearch.co.nz. Right: A lone Mandarin duck, who has chosen to make its home at Lake Rotoiti in Nelson Lakes National Park. This would be an unusual duck to see in a bird survey.

WANT TO DO MORE?

- You can learn more about identifying birds by joining Young Birders, Kiwi Conservation Club or Forest & Bird Youth.
- Birds New Zealand and local restoration groups often need volunteers to count birds.
- Get involved with bird banding. Banding means a bird can be traced, which helps identify how far a bird has flown or how old it is. (See more about banding on page 23).

LANCE RICHDALE
SEABIRD SAVIOUR

Lance Richdale's passion for birds ensured the survival of the toroa/northern royal albatross at Taiaroa Head, on the Otago Peninsula in Dunedin. There is a greater understanding and awareness of hoiho/yellow-eyed penguins because of his work, and he was a pioneer of bird-banding to track birds.

School children in the 1930s knew Lance Richdale as the 'nature study man'. He travelled around schools teaching about nature and farming and growing food. These were fun lessons that the children looked forward to, as they got to spend time outside the classroom making gardens and observing nature. Like all good teachers, Richdale didn't just talk, he listened to the children. It was the children's reports of seeing albatross on Taiaroa Head and yellow-eyed penguins on neighbouring beaches on Otago Peninsula that got him interested in these birds.

Lance Richdale began to spend weekends and holidays camping out to study the toroa and hoiho. Toroa had been seen on Taiaroa Head and some had laid eggs, but locals had collected the eggs, possibly to eat them. Then, in 1935, a chick had hatched, only to be killed by a dog or a stoat. Richdale took up the challenge to protect these birds, not only from pests but also from people, and a fence was built in 1937. When the first two eggs were laid that year, he spent as much time as he could observing and protecting the one surviving chick until it fledged (to have wing feathers large enough for it to fly) in September 1938. This is how the royal albatross colony at Taiaroa Head began.

Lance Richdale also spent many weeks studying hoiho on the Otago Peninsula. He weighed them and took measurements, he noted where they nested, he watched the chicks grow and observed how they behaved towards each other. Realising he needed some way to track individual birds and see if they came back to the same nests, as well as to follow the progress of chicks, he put leg bands on the birds.

His wife Agnes helped with the research, sometimes out at the bird colonies catching and weighing birds and sometimes typing up many pages of research and helping him edit his scientific papers and books. By the 1950s he had become accepted into the science community and was able to get scholarships to help him and Agnes spend more time studying and writing about birds.

Albatross eggs are about 12 centimetres tall.

THREATS TO SEABIRDS

It might seem strange to us now that people collected albatross eggs, but at that time, collecting eggs was a hobby. People just didn't think about how this hobby would affect bird populations. Unfortunately, some people also enjoyed destroying penguin nests and eggs or shooting at the albatross chicks and birds. Another problem for the penguins was a loss of habitat to nest in. Lance Richdale worked hard to educate the public about the birds, writing articles in newspapers and campaigning for their protection.

Lance Richdale with the first northern

ROYAL ALBATROSS COLONY

From the colony's small beginnings of only a few birds in the 1930s, there were 65 breeding pairs and at least 130 non-breeding birds by 2018. In 1967, the Otago Peninsula Trust was formed and some viewing facilities were built. Now the Royal Albatross Centre provides tours and opportunities for people to learn about these amazing birds and the Department of Conservation manages the albatross colony. Lance Richdale died in 1983, the same year the Richdale Albatross Observatory was opened on Taiaroa Head.

Above: Northern royal albatross, Taiaroa Head.
Below: The cliffs below Taiaroa Head.

Lance Richdale wrote scientific books about yellow-eyed penguins but also one for young children called *Podgy the Penguin*.

ALBATROSS & OTHER SEABIRDS

Lance Richdale banded an adult toroa/northern royal albatross in 1937. 'Grandma', as she was later called, survived until 1989. She must have already been a few years old when she was banded, so she is thought to have lived at least 61 years.

In the 1930s, people thought the adult albatross left their chicks without food for months before they fledged, but Lance Richdale's observations showed that adults feed their chicks right up to a few days before they are able to fly. He also observed that the birds came back to meet and breed with the same partner.

A toroa egg takes 80 days to hatch, and the chick needs to grow for about nine months before it is able to fly. Both parents raise the chick, flying out to sea to find food and returning to feed it. Because raising a chick takes so long, they only breed and raise a chick every two years.

Nowadays you can watch toroa on the internet through a web cam, but back then Lance Richdale had to sit in a tent, hut or out in the open for hours to observe the birds. Today it is also possible to track the flight of birds using GPS, but Richdale didn't have this technology, so he could only guess where they went to feed. Data from banded birds and GPS shows us they fly throughout the Southern Ocean, resting on the ocean itself rather than returning to land.

Toroa are classed by scientists in the order *Procellariiformes*, along with prions, petrels and shearwaters. The birds in this order are also commonly called 'tubenoses'. They all have a hole in their beak, through which they can excrete the salt from seawater. Lance Richdale decided to seek out and study seabirds living on Whero, a small, uninhabited island off Stewart Island/Rakiura. Here he was able to observe tītī/sooty shearwaters, tītīwainui/fairy prions, pararā/broad-billed prions, kuaka/common diving petrels, and takahikare-moana/white-faced storm petrels.

The island had so many burrows it made moving around difficult. He visited the island many times, staying for long periods to note when the eggs hatched and the chicks flew away. He weighed birds and banded birds, keeping thorough records. It was the first detailed study of these species.

TOROA FACTS

- Adult toroa weigh about 9 kilograms and have a wing span of over 3 metres.
- They eat squid and other animals that they fish out of the sea with their sharp beaks.
- They are 'tubenose' birds, which means they have an adaptation that allows them to get rid of salt from seawater. The salt dribbles out the hole in their beak.
- Toroa glide on air currents, allowing them to fly for long distances without flapping their wings, as it helps them conserve energy.

Top: Royal albatross soaring above the ocean.
Below: Northern royal albatross and chick, Taiaroa Head, Otago Peninsula.

From left to right: A kororā/little penguin, a hoiho/yellow-eyed penguin, and (illustrated) a tawaki/Fiordland crested penguin.

PENGUINS OF NEW ZEALAND

The three species most commonly found nesting around the mainland of New Zealand are hoiho/yellow-eyed penguins, kororā/little penguins and tawaki/Fiordland crested penguins.

Lance Richdale also had the rare opportunity to study a pair of erect-crested penguins, which nested for at least seven seasons close to the hoiho on the peninsula. Near his study site was a colony of little penguins, and on one occasion a rockhopper penguin was seen and photographed. Erect-crested penguins and rockhopper penguins normally live on New Zealand's subantarctic islands, but they appear on the mainland from time to time.

WHY ARE BIRDS BANDED?

Bands or rings around a bird's legs are used to identify it. Banding native birds can help researchers work out how many of that species of bird there are, where they live, where they fly to, how long they live, and so on. For example, if a banded bird is found a long way from where it was banded or found many years later, this gives scientists important information about where or how long they live.

In total over a million birds have been banded in New Zealand, with over 10,000 birds banded every year. You need permission and training to band native birds. Some Birds New Zealand local branches involve children in bird-banding projects.

Above: If you see a kea with a band, you may be able to find out which kea you have spotted and where it is likely to live by looking up the colour and combination of the bands and/or number at www.keadatabase.nz.
Right: A sparrow being banded.

TAKING ACTION: PROTECTING SHORE & RIVER BIRDS

While hoiho/yellow-eyed penguins make their nests among flax bushes and scrub, little penguins usually build burrows. Little penguins are found around most of the coast of New Zealand. They are very vulnerable to attack from dogs, feral cats and other introduced predators. Nest boxes help keep the chicks safe from cats and dogs, but not from mustelids (weasels, stoats and ferrets). Nest boxes also provide a hiding place for moulting adult penguins.

Many shore birds' nests are at risk from cats, dogs, and other predators. Hedgehogs, for example, can move up to 2 kilometres in one night, eating eggs from shore bird nests along the way. Because shore birds' nests are camouflaged and hard to see, they can also be damaged by people driving cars on beaches. Once disturbed, incubating birds tend to leave their nest, putting the eggs at risk from overheating. Birds that nest along braided rivers face many of the same risks as shore birds.

You can help protect shore and river birds by joining an existing project or starting your own.

ACTIVITY

PROTECTING NESTING SHORE OR RIVER BIRDS

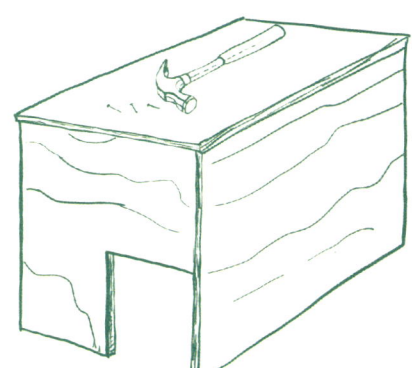

1. Find out which endangered shore or river birds nest near you.
2. Check to see if there is an existing organisation working to protect them and ask if you can help.
3. If you want to take action, here are some other ideas:
   - ✿ Find out as much as you can about when and where the birds breed, and what their biggest threats are.
   - ✿ Let people know through writing signs, leaflets, radio interviews or other campaigns about the dangers to these birds.
   - ✿ Place traps for stoats, hedgehogs and rats around the nesting birds.
   - ✿ Remove weeds and/or plant native plants. Some birds are at risk because of loss of suitable habitat, for example, weeds in river beds where black-billed gulls would usually nest; or not enough plant cover for yellow-eyed penguins to nest among.
   - ✿ If you are targeting blue penguins, build penguin nest boxes out of wood. You will need carpentry skills to do this. You can find instructions online on www.doc.govt.nz or design your own.

Left and above: A kororā/little penguin nesting in a wooden penguin box and another resting in the hollow of a tree in the Marlborough Sounds.

PENGUIN BOXES

In 2016, Te Papa ran a penguin nest-box design challenge. The boxes had to be able to fit four penguins, be weatherproof, keep dogs or other large predators out and be able to be opened by penguin researchers so they could see what was going on inside. The three designs on these pages all met the criteria but you might like to come up with your own design. See www.blog.tepapa.govt.nz for more information.

WANT TO DO MORE?

Look for and report banded birds. Send in a report to the National Banding Office if you find a banded bird and are able to read the bands. If the bird is alive, note down the colour of the bands, reading from left leg to right leg, top to bottom. If it is a metal band, try to see the number on the band (you could use binoculars). If your bird is dead, report the band number, where and when the bird was found, and as many other details as possible.

HELPING INJURED BIRDS

Do you have a local wildlife refuge, bird rescue centre or wildlife hospital? Find out if you can help them. Some bird rescue centres need volunteers, or items such as newspaper and old towels. They may be able to teach you what to do if you ever find an injured bird.

TIP

Read about George Hobson on page 67 and what he's doing for New Zealand's banded dotterels.

BETTY BATHAM

MARINE BIOLOGIST & RESEARCH DIRECTOR

Betty Batham's love of the sea began when she was a child. She was born in Dunedin in 1917, and there were holidays by the sea with her family, plenty of opportunities to explore the shore, and visits to the Fish Hatchery and Marine Investigation Station. She took up photography as a hobby, even developing and printing her own photographs and entering competitions. She was also a talented artist, drawing and painting plants and animals.

In the 1930s she studied at Otago University, one of very few women studying there. She studied home science and English, then switched to botany and zoology. She did very well and was awarded a scholarship to study overseas, but because this was in 1943, she had to wait for the Second World War to finish before she could travel to Cambridge University in England. There she studied sea anemones and was awarded a doctorate. Now she could call herself Dr Batham.

In 1950 she came back to Dunedin to run the Portobello Marine Biological Station on Otago Harbour. At that time, it was quite unusual for a woman to be managing a science facility. The research station had been taken over by Otago University but was quite run-down. There was no road access and no regular ferry service. To get to work on Mondays, Dr Batham paddled across the harbour in her canoe, taking the mail and her food for the week. She paddled back again on Friday afternoons. She worked hard to get funding for a road, not only for herself and her staff but also because she was very keen that children would be able to visit the aquarium to see the seahorses, octopus, sea anemones and other sea creatures on display. The road was built in 1956. And this was just the beginning as then a new laboratory and public aquarium were built.

While Betty Batham's special interest was sea anemones, she thought it was important for people to find out about all the animals that lived around New Zealand shores. 'We're meeting ones we haven't met before almost every day,' she said. It was an exciting time to be involved with marine biology.

Dr Batham took part in many marine expeditions and managed to get funding to purchase a boat for the Marine Biological Station. She also learnt to scuba dive (she was around 50 years old at the time), so she could better understand the environment of the creatures she was studying. As underwater photography was

'Sea anemones, despite their flower-like appearance, are animals of simple structure. They are more advanced than sponges, possessing nerve fibres, which co-ordinate contractions of the muscles. But they have no brains or nerve cords. Like other animals, they eat solid food, and they occasionally slowly walk.'

BETTY BATHAM

In the aquarium, Betty Batham saw an octopus lay eggs on the glass of the tank. Over the next 11 weeks until they hatched, she observed how the mother octopus guarded her eggs and kept the water flowing around them to keep the eggs clean and aerated. She was also able to take photographs through the glass.

still in its early stages, many marine biologists relied on drawing the animals and plants they were studying. She also drew and described many creatures.

Shortly after she resigned from her job as director of the Portobello Marine Biological Station in 1974, she disappeared off the coast of Wellington, presumably in a diving accident.

By the 2000s, the public aquarium buildings that Betty Batham had worked hard to maintain were considered an earthquake risk. A new teaching facility was opened on the site of the old aquarium in 2017.

Common large paua. Grows to 140 mm.

STUDYING THE ROCKY SHORE

Betty Batham studied the rocky shore at Little Papanui on Otago Peninsula, which is exposed to ocean waves that crash against the rocks when they break, and compared it to the relatively calm shore of Otago Harbour by the research station, where the waves are not so strong.

Tides and waves both make a difference to the types of plants and animals that live on the seashore. Marine animals that live between the low-tide and high-tide marks must be able to survive being exposed to the air when the tide goes out and survive being underwater when the tide comes in.

Betty Batham studied the animals and plants that live between the tides, on both shores, to understand how wind, waves and sun affected the types of animals and plants that lived there. She compared the different zones, between the low-tide and high-tide marks, and above the high-tide mark in the 'splash zone'.

Interested to see what differences there are in sea creatures and seaweed between the two places, she found, for example, that bull kelp was common on the wave-exposed shore as were green-lipped mussels, but neither were found in her harbour survey.

The rocky shore, sandy beaches, mudflats and estuaries are important for many reasons. Many people gather food from these areas and expect it to be safe to eat. These areas are also a nursery for some young fish and other creatures. If they can survive in these more protected places, there is a greater chance they will grow to reach adult size and survive out in the ocean. The shore is also important for many shore birds, which rely on these places for food and for nesting.

Knowing the types of animals and plants that are common on the shoreline allows scientists to monitor change over time. Some change is natural, such as how seaweed populations increase or decrease depending on the season. Other change may be caused by human activity, for example changing the shoreline to build roads or wharves or polluting it with sewage or silt (earth that has been washed into the sea).

Building houses near the shore might increase the amount of silt, and surveys can monitor any changes in the number and type of species of shellfish that live in the sand or mud. Monitoring can help answer other questions too, such as what impact climate change is having on the shore and whether fishing or shellfish collection affect the community of animals and plants that live in an area.

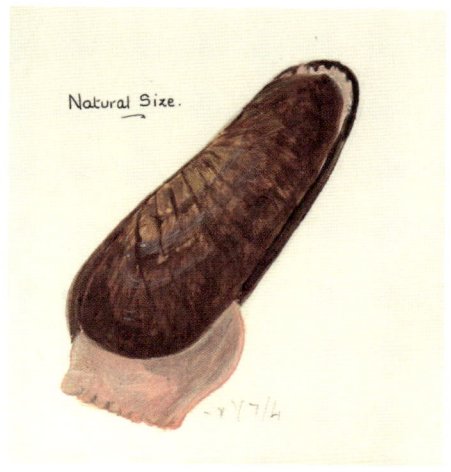

Natural Size.

Above: Two of Betty Batham's drawings that are part of the marine species database she created. Below: Betty (right) is with the crew of the RV *Munida*. One research expedition was to Fiordland, where there are layers of water in a fiord, with freshwater on top as a result of high rainfall, and salty seawater beneath. This creates an unusual habitat where animals live at different depths.

TAKING ACTION: MONITORING THE SHORE

You can become a citizen scientist and collect information about marine life to help scientists and your local community. Monitoring the shore once is useful, but if you come back to the same spot and collect data month after month or year after year, it is even more useful. You can monitor change and investigate the impact of people's activities or weather events on the seashore community.

You can share your data by joining the Marine Metre Squared project (www.mm2.net.nz) run by the New Zealand Marine Studies Centre.

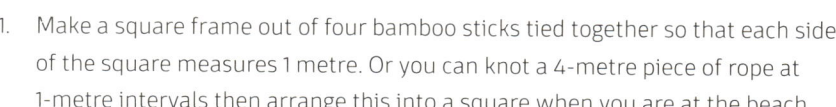

ACTIVITY

TAKING A SHORE SURVEY

You will need:

- a square frame, 1 metre x 1 metre (see instructions below)
- tides timetable
- a guide to identify marine animals: book, leaflet or App
- pen, paper, and a sheet downloaded from the Marine Metre Squared site
- ruler, for placing next to marine life you are photographing
- camera or phone with GPS (optional)
- a tin can with end punctured and an old kitchen sieve, for surveying a mudflat

1. Make a square frame out of four bamboo sticks tied together so that each side of the square measures 1 metre. Or you can knot a 4-metre piece of rope at 1-metre intervals then arrange this into a square when you are at the beach.

2. Plan your trip so it will be low tide at your beach. Look up tide times online or in the newspaper.

3. Choose a place on the shore near the sea and place your square down. Don't turn your back on the waves and do keep an eye on the sea in case the tide starts to come back in.

4. Record the location of your square (you could use GPS on a phone or look it up on Google Maps). You could take a photo that shows where it is in relation to other landmarks and a photo looking down onto the square.

5. Write down which tidal zone you are in: high tide, mid tide or low tide. Look at what the ground (substrate) in your metre square is made of: mud, sand or rock. How much is sand and how much is rock? Your total should come to 100 per cent.

6. How much of the square is covered with seaweed? Write down what percentage is covered by each different seaweed species, for example, completely covered is 100 per cent, half-covered is 50 per cent, quarter-covered is 25 per

TIP

If there is something happening in your community that might affect the beach or ocean, try to do surveys before, during and after. For example, are there plans to build a jetty, create a marine sanctuary, or build houses close to the shore?

cent. Because different seaweed can be piled on top of each other, your total might be more than 100 per cent.

7. Count and identify the animals you can see within the square. Then look for hidden animals under seaweed and rocks. Make sure you keep your feet out of the square and don't try to lift rocks that are too big. If you are counting on the muddy shore, count what is on and what is just under the surface of the mud. Use a tin to take a core sample in each corner. Empty the mud from the core onto a sieve and gently shake in water to remove the sand. Count what animals or plants are in the core sample and use this to estimate how many are in the whole metre square.

8. Share your data by entering it online at www.mm2.net.nz

9. Review your results. How many different types of animals/plants did you find? What animals were most common in your square? How many had shells? Compare your results with any previous surveys. You can also use the website to see what other surveys in your region have found.

WANT TO DO MORE?

Learn how to swim and to snorkel, so you can find out about what lives under the surface of the sea.

DON MERTON

SAVING BIRDS FROM EXTINCTION

Don Merton was born in Auckland in 1939 and grew up in the Gisborne and East Coast area. As a child he was fascinated by birds. One of his favourite books was Pérrine Moncrieff's *New Zealand Birds and How to Identify Them* (see page 14).

When he found a goldfinch nest, he gave some of the eggs to his grandmother's canary to see what would happen and was delighted when the canary raised them. He began raising tame birds such as budgies, but he also spent time observing native and wild birds. One of these birds was the North Island weka. It was already rare in other parts of the North Island and Don Merton realised it could disappear like the huia and the moa. By the time he was 12 years old he decided to devote himself to making sure this couldn't happen.

People from outside his family also began to notice Don Merton's talent with birds and encouraged his interest. Keen bird watchers took him on trips and later, when he was finishing school, he applied to work for the New Zealand Wildlife Service (which became part of the Department of Conservation). His first attempt was unsuccessful, so he went back to school, but his second application was successful and in 1957 he became a Wildlife Service trainee.

Don Merton travelled around the country, including visiting many remote islands. He met other people with the same passion for native birds. One job he had was at Taiaroa Head, where he trapped predators, and he lived in the same hut Lance Richdale had lived in (see page 20). Often he was quite isolated with no transport and only basic rations.

He learnt lots of practical skills, some of which were necessary for his job, such as shooting goats or trapping other introduced wildlife. He also took up photography as a new hobby, which became an important way to document his work.

Sometimes Merton worked alone, but more often he worked in teams. It was important for him to bring together people with different skills and knowledge, such as botanists, technicians who could record bird calls, and conservation dog-handlers.

' The only thing that stood between extinction and survival was us. We learnt the hard way that we were the only ones who could stop something like this happening again.'

DON MERTON

When there are only a few birds left, individuals can be given names. Old Blue was mother of all the Chatham Island black robins that survived to breed successfully. Richard Henry, the name given to the last surviving kākāpō from Fiordland is pictured (below) in Don Merton's arms.

SAVING TĪEKE

By the early 1900s, introduced predators had wiped out tīeke/saddleback on both the North and South islands. The only North Island tīeke were living on Taranga/Hen Island near Whangarei and the only South Island tīeke were on the South Cape Islands near Stewart Island/Rakiura.

In 1963, Don Merton was given the job of creating a second population by moving some from Taranga Island. He knew he first needed to find out more about the birds. He brought together teams of volunteers and scientists to observe the birds on Taranga Island. Some of the volunteers were boys from the King's College Bird Club. They camped on the island and watched the birds, recording what they ate and how they behaved. The observers found that tīeke mostly ate insects, occasionally eating some fruit and nectar. The tīeke preferred forest edges and scrub and found insects in leaf litter on the ground or under tree bark.

Knowing more about the birds made it easier to choose the island they would be transferred to – Whatupuke/Middle Chicken Island. To catch the birds for transfer, their calls were recorded, then the recordings were played back to attract the birds into mist-nets (fine nets that the birds get entangled in). The tīeke were banded and put into an aviary that had been built on the island. To feed the birds, the team collected insects from the forest and also created a maggot farm.

The tīeke were transferred by boat, early in the morning, in darkened, insulated boxes. Twenty-three birds were successfully transferred in 1964 and by the following year they had bred and become established. This was the first successful transfer of birds to protect a species in New Zealand.

It was lucky that Don Merton and his team had figured out how to transfer tīeke because within a few weeks they would need to hurriedly transfer South Island tīeke to a safe place. Māori muttonbirders who visited the South Cape Islands had found the islands were overrun with rats. A few rats must have made it ashore from a ship, and now rats were everywhere, even eating the mattresses and chewing on furniture in buildings.

Don Merton and others took a boat in rough seas to the islands and started work, using the same methods they'd developed for the North Island tīeke. They needed to make new recordings, as the South Island tīeke had a different call. Thirty-six birds were caught and transferred to Big Island and Kaimōhū. While the South Island tīeke survived, other species unfortunately became extinct as a result of the rat invasion of the South Cape Islands, including the tutukiwi/South Island snipe, the greater short-tailed bat and Stead's bush wren. A couple of wrens were transferred but did not survive.

The good news is that North Island tīeke can now be found on 14 islands and 5 mainland sanctuaries. South Island tīeke are on about 20 islands, including the South Cape Islands now that they are free of rats again.

North Island tīeke/saddleback (top) and South Island tīeke/saddleback (below).

TĪEKE/SADDLEBACK FACTS

- Both North and South Island species have orangey-red wattles and orange saddles.
- South Island saddleback juveniles are called jack birds. They are brown all over and don't develop their black plumage and chestnut saddle until they are adults. North Island juveniles do have the chestnut saddle.
- Both species are vulnerable to rats and stoats because of their habit of looking for food on the forest floor or on tree trunks, often hopping around rather than flying, and because they nest in tree holes.

TAKING ACTION: GARDENS FOR NATIVE BIRDS

Observing birds to find out what they ate and where they liked to live was important in saving the tīeke. These same observations are important to make your garden a great place for native birds to live.

Some people put out bird seed for birds, but birds that eat these seeds are mostly introduced birds such as sparrows and finches.

One of the best things you can do for native birds is plant shrubs and trees that provide them with food and shelter. Native birds such as riroriro/grey warbler and pīwakawaka/fantail eat insects. They will be attracted to a garden that has plenty of insects and branches to hide in. Trees or bushes with lots of leaf litter around them make a good place for insects to live.

Kererū eat flowers such as kōwhai, and berries such as pūriri, karaka and tawa. Tūī and korimako/bellbird are nectar eaters. Flowers that provide nectar include harakeke/flax, pōhutukawa, kōwhai and rewarewa (illustrated below).

Above: Tūī perched on a flax in a garden.
Opposite page top: Kakaruia/ black robin
Opposite page below: Tahou/silvereyes feeding.

ACTIVITY

MAKING A SUGAR-FEEDER FOR BIRDS

If you want to feed birds, it is best to do this in winter because in summer there is usually plenty of nectar food around. Sugar-feeders can also attract bees and wasps in summer. Feeding birds occasionally rather than all the time is best, as this means birds are less likely to become dependent on being fed. Remember to keep bird feeders and bird baths clean.

You will need:

☆ a plastic dish (at least 3 cm deep)
☆ wire or string to attach the feeder
☆ strong glue
☆ sugar solution: half a cup of sugar dissolved in 4 cups of water
☆ 1 or 1.5-litre plastic bottle with a lid

1. Find a safe place to put your feeder, out of reach of cats and rats.
2. Attach the lid of your bottle to the centre of the dish.
3. Make some holes about half a centimetre below the bottle neck.
4. Put the sugar solution into the bottle, screw on the lid which is now attached to the dish).
5. Turn the bottle upside down. Some of the sugar solution will come out into the dish up to the level of the holes.
6. Use wire or string to hang the feeder from a tree or attach it to a wooden support. (It is possible to use a glass bottle, but you will need to set it up differently; look online for how to do this.)

You can also put pieces of fruit such as bruised bananas or apples on to a board or feeding table. Secure the fruit with nails so they don't fall off. Make sure the food is out of reach of cats. A bird bath that is placed safely away from cats (at least 1.5 metres high) will be visited by all sorts of birds. Keep the bath clean and the water fresh.

don't forget to poke holes in the bottle!

THINKING LIKE A BIRD

Don Merton is best known for helping save the Chatham Island kakaruia/black robin, as well as the kākāpō, from extinction, but he also worked with many birds, including tīeke/saddleback (both North and South Island), South Island and Chatham Island snipe, and North Island weka. Don Merton also worked overseas, helping to save birds in Mauritius, Seychelles, Christmas Island and Australia. Much of Don's time was spent in the field, capturing birds, building aviaries, raising chicks and working out practical solutions to the many problems encountered in saving wildlife from extinction. His childhood experience of fostering chicks and letting them be raised by other birds helped him years later when he was faced with the problem of there being less than ten Chatham Island black robins still alive. He did this by using other birds to foster black robin chicks, which then encouraged the black robin parents to lay a second lot of eggs.

DID YOU KNOW?

Some foods are bad for birds and can cause death or severe illness. This includes feeding bread to ducks and nuts to kākā. Check which are appropriate kinds of bird food.

WANT TO DO MORE?

If you have a cat, find out how to keep it from catching birds. A bell on its collar can work by alerting birds to the cat's presence, or better still keep your cat indoors.

GEORGE GIBBS

WĒTĀ EXPERT

A love of insects runs in George Gibb's family. His grandfather, George Hudson, was one of New Zealand's leading early naturalists, who produced many books of his superb paintings of insects. George Hudson encouraged his young grandson by giving him little boxes of insects and containers for his own collections. George's mother (Hudson's daughter) helped keep this interest in insects alive after his grandfather died. Family trips were often to wild places, tramping, camping or cycling, and these gave George opportunities to learn about different insects.

Studying insects and other animals at university (zoology) was the next step for George Gibbs. However, at university in the 1950s, the study of zoology usually focused on studying dead animals, compared to the study of ecology, which studied living animals in their habitats and seeing how species interact. Ecology made sense to George Gibbs and he kept studying, spending some years in Australia researching the ecology of fruit flies.

George Gibbs then returned to Victoria University in Wellington as a lecturer in ecology. He took students on field trips and encouraged their interests, and together they researched New Zealand's animals, particularly insects. One of his students, Mary Morgan Richards (now a professor at Massey University), was very interested in wētā. George realised how little was known about New Zealand's largest insect and he, too, became fascinated by the mysteries of giant wētā and began researching them.

There seemed to be very few giant wētā left. George Gibbs explains: 'New Zealand had a lot of big insects and other invertebrates such as snails. They are wonderful food for birds but also for rats and other predators, so they have had a tough time.'

George began trying to answer the questions of where New Zealand's plants and animals originally came from and how animals like wētā first got to New Zealand. Some geologists started to talk about the possibility of New Zealand once having been submerged completely under the sea. It's a theory that's now been disproved, but at the time it made people wonder how wētā got to New Zealand. Gibbs taught a course on the origin of New Zealand plants and animals, and this led him to write a detailed book on this topic called *Ghosts of Gondwana*. Now that he's retired from teaching, George Gibbs has also written a biography of his grandfather.

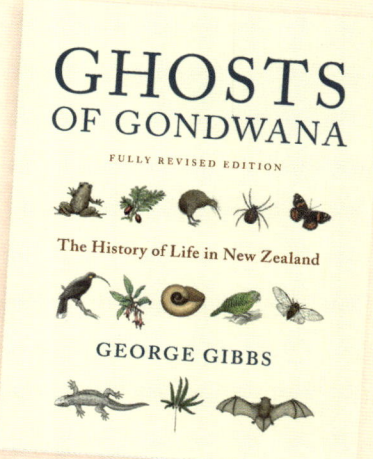

GEORGE GIBBS' GRANDFATHER, GEORGE HUDSON

Born in London in 1867, George Hudson arrived in New Zealand with his family on a sailing ship when he was 14. He worked at the post office, spending his spare time collecting, studying and painting New Zealand's insects. Being an entomologist was the major focus of his life. He wrote and illustrated many books about butterflies and moths and other New Zealand insects.

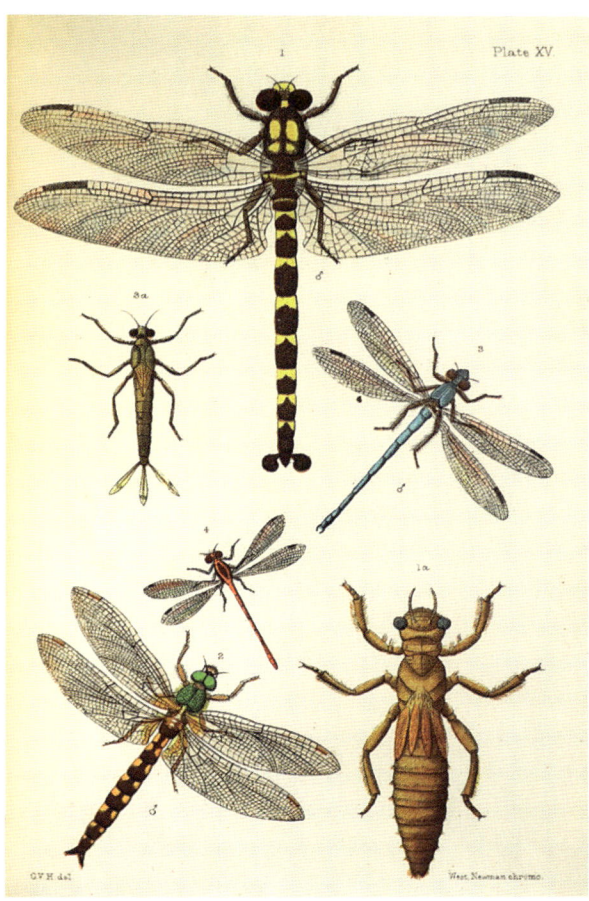

Examples of George Hudson's beautiful and meticulous paintings of New Zealand insects.

COLLECTING INSECTS

Entomologists (people who study insects) need to build up collections of insects. This usually means killing them and preserving them. A museum collection that is well looked after and carefully labelled can continue to provide answers about insects for many years. Often new species are discovered this way.

Field trips to collect insects require a lot of organisation, and equipment includes traps, nets and torches. There are also boxes of tubes and alcohol for preserving. Every find has to be carefully labelled with where and when it was found. Today, people use GPS locations, so the findings can be mapped accurately.

BIOGEOGRAPHY

The word 'biogeography' combines 'biology' and 'geography'. It is the study of how plants and animals come to be living in different parts of the world. This study collects clues from fossils, DNA studies and geological changes over time. For example, insects in the wētā family can be found in New Zealand, Africa, Australia and South America – all once part of Gondwana, the ancient supercontinent from which all of these landmasses broke off, many millions of years ago. Therefore, an ancestor of wētā would most likely have lived on Gondwana, alongside dinosaurs and many other ancient creatures.

The giant wētāpunga (left) and the tusked Raukumara (right). Only the male Raukumara have tusks. The illustration below is of the Bluff wētā.

SEARCHING FOR WĒTĀ

While wētā are found in other countries, there are over 100 species of wētā in New Zealand, which makes New Zealand a wētā hot spot. The wētā that people most often see are tree wētā. They are commonly found in gardens and their aggressive behaviour has helped them survive better than some other wētā. The other wētā groups include cave wētā, of which there are over 50 species, ground wētā, tusked wētā and giant wētā. The rarest are tusked and giant wētā (wētāpunga).

While investigating giant wētā, George Gibbs became interested in some old museum specimens. These wētā had been collected and preserved in alcohol, yet nobody knew anything about them. In fact, some people assumed they were from a species now extinct. One bottle label showed that the giant wētā had been found at Mt Somers in Canterbury, and it named the person who had found it.

The first search for a living giant wētā of this species was not successful. After a bit of detective work and a phonecall to the person who found it, a second search got underway. Knowing that similar wētā from Kaikōura live in rock crevices, a 1994 search party to find them included a rock climber. This was the key, and over half a dozen were found among the rocks that day, proving that this species was not extinct.

Another discovery, about 20 years ago, was of the Raukumara tusked wētā. A hunter working for DOC discovered and killed a tusked wētā while he was cleaning up a hut. He was curious enough to keep it. When George Gibbs saw the dead wētā, he realised it was a new species. An expedition to find out more about this wētā was organised. The hut in the Raukumara area (East Coast, North Island) was difficult to get to, but when George and the others finally arrived, they did a night-time search and were amazed to find this wētā species everywhere.

Wētā play an important role in the food web of an ecosystem, and studying these invertebrates helps scientists work out whether an ecosystem is healthy. They are important food for tuatara and ruru/morepork who hunt at night. During the daytime, other birds such as kākā and tīeke can find them by pulling away bark and exposing their hiding places.

Tree and giant wētā are mostly vegetarian, but tusked wētā and ground wētā are carnivorous, eating moths and other invertebrates.

GIANT INSECTS

The largest of all the giant wētā is the wētāpunga, which can weigh up to 35 grams. It was initially found all over Northland but survived only on Hauturu/ Little Barrier Island, where there were no European rats. Because giant wētā make an easy meal for introduced mammal predators such as rats, today most species only survive on predator-free islands or high in the Southern Alps, above the rat-infested lowlands.

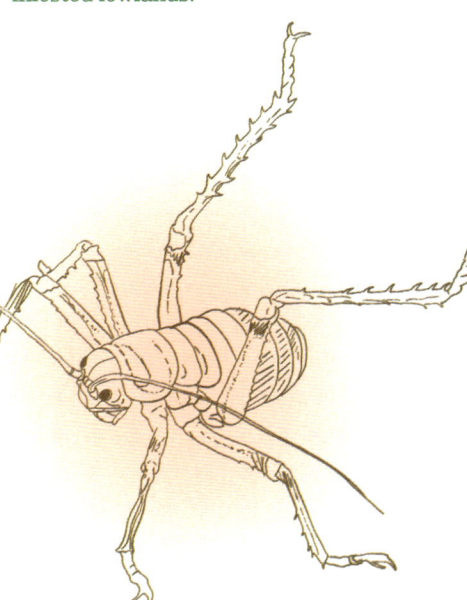

MORE WĒTĀ FACTS

- Wētā are nocturnal.
- Wētā need to moult (shed their exoskeleton) in order to grow. A tree wētā needs to moult nine times before it gets to adult size.
- Wētā let off a strong smell, which makes it easier to find each other.
- Some alpine wētā can survive being frozen and then thawed.
- Some wētā live alone, but tree wētā often live together in large groups.

TAKING ACTION: MAKING A HOME FOR WĒTĀ

Because wētā are large insects they can be easy to study and count. Being able to see how many are living in an area of bush that has been replanted or restored is a good way to see how successful the project has been at creating a healthy ecosystem. You can build and use a wētā 'motel' to monitor and count them. Tree wētā don't make their own tunnels, they use holes made by other insects or by people, and they like to huddle together into groups. Your wētā motel will keep wētā safe from rats and other mammal predators. Of course other creatures might like your wētā motel too. Sometimes spiders or geckos might move in for a while.

TIP

New Zealand comes alive at night, so it is a good time to go looking for insects such as wētā and moths. Take a torch to see what's living in a particular tree, flax bush or other parts of your garden. Other invertebrates you might find include spiders, snails and slugs.

ACTIVITY

DESIGNING & BUILDING A WĒTĀ 'MOTEL'

Decide on the purpose of your project. Do you want to make a safe haven for wētā? Or do you also want to monitor and study your wētā? There are many different designs available online. The simplest wētā house is a piece of hollow bamboo that hangs, so the opening is underneath and the top is sealed. Many are made of wood to imitate a tree cavity, but a piece of closed cell foam wrapped around a tree trunk to mimic bark would also work. If you want to be able to see the wētā, you will need to create a door that you can open.

Things to think about in your design:

- ✿ A wētā cavity that would be big enough to hold a group of tree wētā is 80 x 50 x 25 millimetres.
- ✿ Entrance holes should be 16 millimetres in diameter and slope upwards so the rain can't get in.
- ✿ Wētā will not live inside the cavity if light gets in during the day.
- ✿ Some wētā motels have perspex over the holes so wētā don't fall out and you can view the wētā when the cover is lifted. However, perspex can make the holes too damp because condensation builds up, so make sure air can circulate around.
- ✿ If you are using closed cell foam, an A3-sized piece is probably large enough.

Placement of your motel:

- ✿ Put it on a tree out of sunlight and where rainwater can't get in.
- ✿ Wētā are more likely to use a hole/home that smells of wētā, so look for wētā poo to smear inside.

WANT TO DO MORE?

- Do an insect census in your garden using a pitfall trap. This is a container with smooth sides, buried, so its top is level with the ground (for example, the lower half of a plastic bottle). Insects will fall into the trap and can then be counted. Leave a stick in the trap when you aren't using it, so animals can climb out.
- Build a bug motel for other insects and invertebrates to live in. Stack a few pieces of wood using bricks to create spaces. Fill these with found materials such as small lengths of bamboo, pieces of bark stacked up, tightly packed twigs, pine cones and so on.

INGRID VISSER

FRIEND OF AOTEAROA'S ORCA

Dr Ingrid N. Visser began studying New Zealand's orca in the 1990s. She made some important discoveries about the New Zealand orca population, which has helped with their protection. Now she studies orca (also called killer whales) all over the world, and campaigns to free them from captivity.

As a child, Ingrid Visser learnt to snorkel in a paddling pool in her backyard, but now as an adult she has snorkelled and dived with orca all around the world. Ingrid always knew she wanted to work with whales and dolphins, however, it was when she was studying marine biology in Auckland that she had a chance meeting with David Attenborough, world famous for his nature documentaries. She describes this meeting in her autobiography. She told him she wanted to go and study the orca in South America that had been featured in his documentaries. He asked her why she didn't work on the New Zealand orca, and Ingrid says, 'I was stumped – it just hadn't occurred to me this would be a possibility.'

Making this her goal, Ingrid Visser worked hard to get sponsors who would fund the equipment she needed to start her research, including a camera, a boat and a 4WD vehicle. She contacted scientists working with orca in other parts of the world and realised that identifying individual orca was the vital first step. Orca are identified from their dorsal fin, as well as the pigmentation markings on the side of their heads and a grey patch behind the fin called the saddle patch.

She asked the public to send in information and photographs about any orca they had seen. She also asked people to call her as soon as they saw orca, so that, if they were near her, she could take her boat out to see them and take photos. Soon she was starting to notice the same orca appearing in different places around New Zealand.

By matching sightings to her photo database, Ingrid was able to work out that there were only around 200 orca in New Zealand waters. This, along with some of her other findings, gave the Department of Conservation enough information to put the species on the list of 'nationally critical' animals, which means they are at risk of extinction.

Ingrid Visser established the Orca Research Trust, which continues to study New Zealand's orca. The trust also campaigns to free orca that are being kept captive in theme parks for people's entertainment.

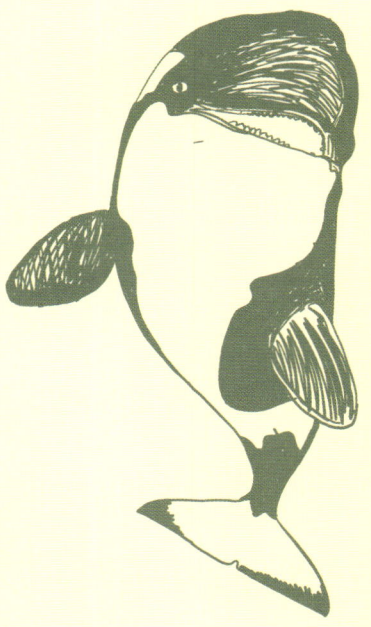

ORCA IN CAPTIVITY

Over 60 orca are held captive in theme parks around the world, where they must perform tricks to entertain people, and to get fed. Many more have died, either in captivity or in people's attempts to capture them. Keeping orca in captivity is controversial because they are highly intelligent animals and suffer from not having the space they would in the wild and from being separated from their family groups.

IDENTIFYING ORCA

Orca are amazing mammals. Sometimes described as wolves of the ocean, they are apex predators, which means they are at the top of the food chain. They prey on other animals such as dolphins, sharks and stingrays, but nothing preys on them unless they are injured or sick.

At up to 9 metres long and weighing up to 5.5 tonnes, they are an awesome sight in the ocean. Despite being a top predator, there are no known attacks on humans by orca in the wild, although captive orca have attacked and killed trainers and others who enter their tanks.

Orca are known to live for a long time. Females can live up to 80 or 90 years and males up to 50 or 60 years. They live in family groups, pods, and hunt together.

Ingrid Visser's research has identified family groupings around New Zealand, as well as different subspecies of orca. For example, she found that one group stays around the North Island, a second one is found around the South Island, and a third group travels around both the North and South islands. One surprise is that Antarctic orca are sometimes seen around New Zealand's coast.

Different groups can have different hunting techniques that they pass on from generation to generation. Ingrid Visser discovered that some of New Zealand's orca hunt stingrays and eagle rays. They need to avoid the stingray's barb, and they do this by flipping the stingray over so it can't move. It is still risky, however, and young orca need to be taught this by the adults. New Zealand orca also prey on six different species of sharks, and occasionally on dolphins.

Sometimes orca get stranded when they chase rays into shore. Orca have been successfully rescued from strandings and have gone on to live for many years. The Department of Conservation is responsible for managing any whale or dolphin strandings, but anyone can help rescue a stranded mammal if they are physically able. Ingrid Visser works closely with the department to increase the chances of survival of stranded orca.

Orca are also at risk of injury from boats. Some of the markings used to identify individual orca have been caused by injuries from the spinning blades of propellers.

HELPING STRANDED ORCA

If you find a stranded orca (or other marine mammal):

- Call the DOC hotline 0800 362 468 and the Orca Hotline 0800 SEE ORCA (733 6722).
- Follow the instructions of DOC staff.
- It is important to keep the stranded animal calm – don't startle them or make loud noises; keep dogs and small children away.
- Ensure it is kept cool by pouring water on it, but remember, like us, animals breathe air, so don't pour water down a whale's blowhole!
- Make sure you keep yourself safe, keep hydrated and wear sunblock, and don't go out of your depth.
- If you are over 15 and live or holiday near a beach where animals are often stranded, you might like to do a Project Jonah course.

Orca can grow up to 9 metres in length. Male orca have tall dorsal fins, sometimes up to 1 metre high.

TAKING ACTION: CONTRIBUTING TO MARINE MAMMAL RESEARCH

Have you seen orca or other marine mammals, such as whales? If you go out on boats or live in areas where orca or whales are sometimes seen from the coast, you can contribute to research by reporting sightings.

ACTIVITY

REPORTING AN ORCA SIGHTING

Sometimes you might be lucky to see orca. If you do, contact the Orca Research Trust on the Orca Hotline 0800 SEE ORCA (733 6722) as soon as you see them. The Research Trust may be able to get there quickly and identify the animals before they move on. Otherwise, collect information and report these details to the Orca Research Trust. Reliable information and photos can help the Trust identify the orca you've sighted using their database.

INFORMATION TO COLLECT:

- ☆ Date and time
- ☆ Where were you? Include GPS data if possible (smart phones can give you a GPS position even if there is no phone reception)
- ☆ How far away from the animals were you?
- ☆ If you were on a boat, how far from land were you?

KEEPING ORCA SAFE AT SEA

The New Zealand government has created laws to keep marine mammals (and people) safe. People must respect orca and not harass or disturb them. Some of the rules include:

- Do not swim with orca.
- Boats should not get closer than 50 metres, and there should be no more than three boats within 300 metres.
- Boats should move slowly and quietly at 'no wake' speed and not circle or cut through the group.
- Never drive your boat in front of the group and always depart at a slow speed.

Ingrid Visser tending to a stranded orca.

* ☆ What was the water temperature and how deep was the water?
* ☆ How many animals were in the pod?
* ☆ Did you see any adult males or any calves?
* ☆ Were there any orca with distinctive fins, for example, scarred, bent or unusually shaped?
* ☆ What behaviour did you see? For example, were the animals swimming, breaching, diving, showing their tails or hunting?
* ☆ What direction were they travelling in?

TAKING PHOTOS SHOWING ORCA MARKINGS

Try to capture these areas in your photos: dorsal fin, saddle patch and eye patch.

* **Hold the camera steady.** Taking good photos on a boat can be difficult, especially if it is moving about. Sit down or brace yourself against part of the boat so you can hold the camera as still as possible. If the camera has a strap put it around your neck. A waterproof case for a phone camera is a good idea as well.
* **Use video mode.** Depending on your camera you might not be fast enough or close enough to get a good photo of the markings. To avoid lots of blurred photos, consider taking a video; you may be able to use a video 'still' to see the markings. If you can't take photos you might still be able to do a quick sketch with pen and paper of the animal's markings.
* **How long is your boat?** Find out how long your boat is in metres and this should help you estimate the length of the orca by comparing it to the length of the boat.

WANT TO DO MORE?

* You can post photos and observations of wildlife on iNaturalistNZ. Many scientists use these observations to learn more about the animals they are studying.
* You can use the Hector's Dolphin Sightings App to report sighting of Hector's and Maui's dolphins as well as other marine mammals. This information goes to the Department of Conservation.
* Plastic rubbish in the ocean endangers orca and other marine wildlife. You can help marine wildlife by using less plastic and by picking up rubbish on beaches and around rivers. See also organising a beach clean-up on page 64.

MIRIAM RITCHIE

CONSERVATION DOG-HANDLER

Miriam Ritchie grew up at Matapouri Bay in Northland, near the Poor Knights Islands. It was a remote place when she was a child, with unsealed roads and not many visitors. Growing up, she spent time out at the Poor Knights with her marine biologist father and biology teacher mother, and later helped her dad on his charter boat. All that boating experience has come in handy, as many of the places where she now works are sanctuary islands that can only be reached by boat.

Miriam Ritchie was already working for the Department of Conservation when she became involved with pest-detection dogs. She was removing weeds on Raoul Island, which is part of the Kermadec Island group to the north of New Zealand, at the same time that feral cats and rats were being eradicated. Here she got the opportunity to first work with a cat-detection dog, and then a rat-detection dog called Pipi. By the time she came back to the mainland, she was hooked on this type of work.

Now, Miriam has four pest detection dogs, Ahu, Will, Moss and Woody, and a retired pig dog called Plague. She works as a dog handler in the New Zealand Conservation Dogs Programme, managed by the Department of Conservation, and visits pest-free islands and sanctuaries to help keep them free of mice, rats and stoats. She loves training and working with her dogs. 'It's so rewarding. You get them as a pup and watch them grow. By the time they're about five or six years old, they are just amazing – awesome, wise, well-behaved dogs. You get to know each other so well.'

Being a dog handler requires a lot of dedication. It's a 24-hour, 7 days a week job. If the dogs find a rat scent in her woodshed at home, she can't just ignore it or tell them off, for example, but needs to encourage them and praise them for finding the rat scent. The dogs also need to keep their skills fresh and need regular training between jobs. 'You need to be an outdoors person, happy to walk up hills all day and be prepared to work hard.'

Miriam now uses her experience to test other dogs and their handlers to make sure they are ready to work as conservation dogs. Dogs and their handlers have to pass two tests before they are certified. Handlers also have to show they know how to look after their dogs, and that they understand the behaviour of the pests they are going to be tracking down.

A DOG'S SENSE OF SMELL

The Conservation Dogs Programme takes advantage of a dog's incredible sense of smell. Dogs have:

- separate air passages for breathing and smelling
- nostrils that can smell independently, which makes it easier for them to identify which direction the smell comes from
- hundreds of millions more smell receptors (cells for receiving smells) than humans
- a much larger part of their brain devoted to processing smells than humans – in fact it's around 40 times larger
- a 'vomeronasal organ' which helps them smell things we can't. This helps them detect things such as if people are unwell.

WHAT IS BIOSECURITY?

As well as looking for pests in sanctuaries and on islands, Miriam Ritchie and her dogs do biosecurity work – they check people's luggage, cargo and any boats going out to sanctuary islands to make sure they are free of pests. They also check the marinas the boats used and were moored at before travelling to these islands. Boaties and island visitors need to do their own checks, too, so there is even less chance of a rat, mouse or other pest getting to a pest-free island.

'Dogs are pack animals, and they want a pack leader. They want to know where they stand. You have to be quite clear with them as pups so they know what's right and wrong, and that can be tricky if they are super cute (which they always are!), but you know if you put in the discipline, they'll be amazing dogs.'

MIRIAM RITCHIE

CONSERVATION DOGS

A pest-detection dog wants to find pests, but the humans working with the dog would rather not find any. This is because if pests are found on a pest-free island or within a fenced sanctuary, this is very expensive to fix. Apart from the likely death of endangered wildlife, it could also mean having to move these animals out of the sanctuary and protect them somewhere else until the pest is eradicated. This is many hours of hunting and trapping.

Miriam Ritchie and her rat-detection dog Moss were sent to Waikawa/Portland Island off the Mahia Peninsula in Hawke's Bay, to find out what had killed a large number of rare shore plover birds. Both a cat-detection dog and a stoat-detection dog had already visited the island and had not been able to find anything. Waikawa has mice on it and, as Moss is also trained to find mice, Miriam still had to praise him whenever he found a mouse or mouse scent, so it made for a long, slow process working her way around the island. She and Moss were there for four days. Luckily, Miriam can usually tell the difference in Moss's reaction between mice and rats.

Clever Moss eventually found what looked like a rat burrow with a stash of dead birds nearby. Miriam noted the GPS location, took photographs and also took some material back to be tested. The tests showed that a rat had been there. This was too late for the birds already dead, but it gave the ranger on the island information that would help catch the rat if it were still alive and to hopefully prevent more rats arriving.

Terriers make good pest-detection dogs, because they have a strong hunting instinct. They wear a muzzle so they can't hurt the protected species they are working around. As pups they learn some basic rules, such as not chasing

Miriam Ritchie and her dogs returning from Mana Island.

rabbits, coming when called, and not to jump on people. Then at six months they start learning other obedience skills as well as learning about the animal they are going to target. The training starts by using dead animals, because it is important the dogs learn to find any pests, dead or alive. Their trainer teaches them to 'indicate' when they find a scent of the target animal. Once they've passed their interim obedience test, they are allowed on to conservation land. They still have lots to learn as they will encounter all sorts of other creatures such as penguins, seals or kiwi, and so they have to learn to focus just on their target species.

Other dog breeds, such as pointers, setters and Labradors, can be trained to find threatened native bird species such as kiwi or whio, so these birds can be managed and protected. These dogs are also in the Conservation Dogs Programme.

TAKING ACTION: LEAVE NO TRACE

One of the main ways that pests get into sanctuaries or on to islands is by people. Rats might have stowed away on a boat or mice might have found their way into a backpack or sleeping bag. Other pests can be carried on our shoes or clothes, such as the organism that causes kauri dieback or the deposits of seeds of weeds.

Our behaviour also has an impact on the place we visit, for example, a camp fire can turn into a forest fire or rubbish we leave on the beach might end up in the ocean. There is a worldwide Leave No Trace movement, which is in New Zealand, too. The idea is that if we all take care, we can retain wilderness (and the animals that live there) and other places for all to enjoy.

You can learn how to leave no trace from your visit to a wild place or sanctuary. Some places have particular instructions that you need to follow and your gear might even be inspected. But in other places you visit, it will be up to you and your group to ensure you leave no trace.

KEEPING YOUR DOG UNDER CONTROL

Dogs that aren't trained or controlled can be a danger to wildlife. Unfortunately, dogs have been known to kill kiwi and penguins and other wildlife. For this reason, there are parks and reserves where dogs are not allowed or where they must be kept on a lead. But even where these rules don't apply, it is still important to control your dog.

- Make sure your dog can obey simple commands.
- Keep it in sight.
- Carry a leash and use it when necessary, for example, if you encounter fur seals on a beach or to ensure other people are able to enjoy the area.
- Don't let your dog chase birds.
- Clean up after your dog.

TRAINING DOGS

- Use positive reinforcement, praise and reward your dog when it does what you want.
- Decide on the commands and rules you want your dog to follow and be consistent.
- Keep training sessions short and simple.
- Be patient.
- Find out more about dog training from SPCA, books, videos, or join a local puppy class.

PLANNING A TRIP TO LEAVE NO TRACE

You will need:

- ✩ access to the internet, maps and other information about the place
- ✩ ziplock bags or sealable containers
- ✩ good brushes for cleaning clothes and shoes
- ✩ cleaning materials

Trip to Island sanctuary
Check: all our gear for pests
Clean: our footwear and gear.
Seal: pack our food in containers with lids or seals.

1. 'Leave No Trace' can be applied to any outdoor activity, for example, visiting a sanctuary, tramping, camping, fishing, mountain biking. Find out whether there are any special conditions for visiting. Is it a sanctuary? A place where dogs aren't allowed? Is there Didymo in the river? Are there kauri trees?

2. Look at and know the Leave No Trace principles:

   Plan ahead and prepare: *Kia tika mai te mahere, i mua i te haerenga*
   Travel and camp on durable ground: *Kaua koe e kōtiti i ngā arahikoi, kia tika mai koe te wāhi, hopuni ai.*
   Dispose of waste properly: *Kaua koe e tukinotia i a Papatuānuku.*
   Leave what you find: *Kaua koe e raweketia ngā wāhi tapu, me ngā wāhi motuhake rānei.*
   Minimise the effects of fire: *Me tupato koe ki ngā ariā o te ahi.*
   Respect wildlife and farm animals: *Me kauanuanu koe ki ngā kararehe katoa.*
   Be considerate of others: *Me whaiwhakaaro koe, ki ētahi atu*

3. Plan ahead and prepare. Think about what you will need on your trip. What are the conditions of the place? For example, if you are going to an area with kauri trees, check whether the track is open, shoes will need to be cleaned, and so on. Talk with the others in your group about how you will follow the principles. How will your group dispose of waste properly? You might make sure someone is responsible for carrying out any rubbish; you might agree on using toilets provided in campgrounds; you may need to take a small spade and make sure everyone knows how and where to bury poo.

4. Create a checklist for everyone in the group before you begin. Include a list of things to take, as well as ideas on how to follow the Leave No Trace principles.

WANT TO DO MORE?

Dogs shouldn't be taken into areas where there are kiwi. If you do live in an area near kiwi, or you have hunting dogs, you should take your dog to kiwi-avoidance training. Perhaps you might like to attend a Leave No Trace Awareness workshop, or organise one for a group you belong to.

TIPS

Cleaning shoes. Remove any mud or dirt by brushing or washing. Apply disinfectant or a bleach solution to kill off any organisms. Cleaning clothes and gear. Make sure clothes are washed; check socks, Velcro and all pockets for any seeds or other vegetation clinging to them.
In the South Island, if you are visting an area where there is Didymo in rivers, avoid spreading it by following the 'Didymo Check, Clean, Dry' guidelines.
In the North Island, in areas with kauri, avoid contributing to kauri dieback. Clean your shoes at home and also at any cleaning stations. Keep on tracks. Don't walk on tracks that are closed.

PĀTAKA MOORE & CALEB ROYAL

RIVER KAITIAKI

Pātaka Moore (left) and Caleb Royal.

Pātaka Moore and Caleb Royal are working together to restore their ancestral waterways. They are both Ngāti Raukawa and were born and brought up in Ōtaki. Their ancestors lived here before them and their roots are in this place. Although both of them went away to university, they were drawn back home. They knew of each other at school and are distantly related, but they are a few years apart in age, so it wasn't until they returned from university they discovered their common interest in working to restore the local environment.

Caleb Royal credits his grandfather for inspiring him, along with an 'awesome teacher' who brought science to life. At first Caleb thought he'd study marine biology but along the way freshwater biology took over. Now he and Pātaka Moore are teachers themselves, teaching Kaitiakitanga (guardianship and protection), Environmental Management at Te Wānanga o Raukawa in Ōtaki.

Pātaka Moore's parents were always keen on him going to university, and he feels a strong obligation to use his education to look after the environment. 'It's our responsibility to look after our streams now, as the situation with our polluted streams is shocking. We need to pass on to our kids streams that are in a better condition than they are now. It's a pretty tall order.'

Caleb Royal agrees. 'It's so hard. A lot of species have been teetering on the brink of extinction for such a long time, and that's when we notice them, so by the time you get on to this, you are working with something that's just hanging on.'

This sense of responsibility also shows in their determination to base their work on the values of their ancestors and kaumātua. They wanted to look at the health of streams through a Māori perspective and to be able to answer their community's questions, such as 'Is it safe to swim in?' or 'Is the kai safe to eat?'

Part of their work is getting people to change the way they see waterways. Because we get our food from supermarkets and water from taps, it's easy to forget the importance of streams and rivers in our lives. And it's all too easy for people to think that it's okay to divert or modify rivers, forgetting there is a whole ecosystem living in that waterway.

One of the streams they are trying to restore is the Mangapouri Stream, which winds through the Ōtaki township.

> 'A stream has a cycle within it, natural processes, small insects, kōura and fish that help to keep it clean. If we upset the balance, we aren't allowing the stream to operate as a stream.'
>
> **PĀTAKA MOORE**

Mangapouri Stream, Ōtaki.

MANGAPOURI STREAM RESTORATION

Caleb Royal remembers how his grandad kept a tuna/eel box in the stream at the end of the garden, and in the 1980s, the gentle flow of the stream kept cool, clear water running through. 'As a kid we used to swim in it, dam it up with stones, make little bathing pools. We'd climb through the culverts and go wandering upstream, and we'd catch dozens and dozens of kōura. There was always heaps and heaps of tuna in there as well.' Now, Mangapouri Stream is one of the most polluted rivers in the Wellington region. It's no longer safe to swim in, the kōura have all gone and it's full of noxious weeds and silt.

Left: Students investigating their local river in Nelson.

UNCOVERING THE MANGAPOURI STREAM HISTORY

Pātaka Moore and Caleb Royal interviewed kaumātua about the stream's history, gathering stories about what used to live in the stream, how it was used, and how it has changed. They also used old photographs and maps to uncover changes. They found that the Mangapouri Stream was once the heart of Ōtaki.

In the 1800s, mills were built on the stream, using the power of water to drive waterwheels. Households took water from the stream and used it for gathering and storing food. But as time moved on, people valued the stream less for water and food and more as a way to get rid of rubbish or channel stormwater away. Like many other streams around New Zealand, Mangapouri Stream was also partly re-routed, its direction changed to suit urban development.

The Mangapouri Stream has its source in a spring near the Ōtaki township. It then winds its way behind houses, under a school, and on towards the sea. The project to restore the stream started with research, gathering data about fish numbers and measuring water quality.

Pātaka Moore and Caleb Royal then needed to find out where the pollution was coming from. They realised one of the biggest problems for the Mangapouri Stream is stormwater. Heavy rain pours into drains, carrying with it dog poo, oil from roads, rubbish and dirt. The drains, which are part of the town's stormwater system, empty all this into the stream.

There are other problems for the stream. As it travels unfenced through some farms, it is easy for stock to get into the stream, and as it travels behind people's gardens, it is used as a dumping ground. Some of the pollutants increase the level of nutrients in the water, which causes weeds to grow rapidly. Weeds slow the water-flow down, then soil or dirt that has been washed in gets caught in the weeds, silting up the stream where stones would have been.

In some places, the stream is piped or goes through culverts. This makes it hard for migrating fish to journey upstream.

Knowing the stream's problems was an important step, but the key was finding out what the stream had been like in the past (see page 47). This helped them understand what the stream should be like and how it should behave.

As stormwater is the big issue because of pollution and because it changes the water flow so much, the men continue to work with the council and property developers on trying to control the amount of stormwater that enters the stream. However, replanting along the stream banks and fencing off parts of the stream wouldn't be enough to help the stream return to how it was in the past. They needed to engage the local community to take more responsibility for the stream. The plan is for the community to regularly remove the noxious weeds, which is currently done by contractors. This gives the locals a chance to reconnect with their stream.

TAKING ACTION: LOOKING AFTER OUR WATERWAYS

Unfortunately, there are many rivers, streams, ponds, lakes and wetlands around New Zealand that are affected by human activities. If you want to help look after a waterway, find out if there are local projects already underway that you can join. Here are two activities you can do to help an existing project or to start your own.

ACTIVITY

STOPPING STORM-WATER POLLUTION

Water that empties into drain systems in cities and towns has to go somewhere. Often it empties into streams, rivers or harbours, taking with it pollution and rubbish. Some of the problems include: people washing cars in driveways and the soapy water going into drains, people tipping paint down drains, rubbish such as plastic bags and takeaway containers getting washed off roads and footpaths into drains.

YOU COULD:

☆ Investigate in your neighbourhood where the water in the local drains goes and find out what other problems there are.

☆ Create a campaign to draw attention to where the stormwater goes and find a way to highlight the drains.

☆ Find what other solutions there are to stormwater problems. Maybe there are some innovative ideas being used where you live, for example, some developers are using swales: wide ditches with plants to absorb and filter rainwater rather than have it run off straight into streams.

Below: Children painting around local drains (with water-safe paint) to highlight that all water in drains goes to the sea.

UNDERSTANDING YOUR LOCAL WATERWAY

Every stream, river, lake or wetland has a different history. Finding out about the history of a waterway can help with restoration projects.

YOU COULD:

☆ Interview local elders about their memories of the waterway.
How did they use it? What animals lived here? How has it changed?
Do they have photographs of it? What stories did their ancestors tell about it?

☆ Visit your local museum to find out more information, look for old photographs and maps.

☆ Ask local historians if the waterway was mentioned in historical accounts, for example, books, journals.

☆ Search paperspast.natlib.govt.nz for news items that mention your waterway and digitalnz.org for photographs and maps.

☆ Share what you find with local environmental groups or your council.

WANT TO DO MORE?

☆ Learn about making fish ladders to help fish migrate upstream.

☆ See page 66–67 to find out what Brandon Intermediate Enviro Team is doing to restore their local streams.

☆ Find out how to restore estuary banks to make suitable habitat for īnanga/whitebait to lay their eggs.

☆ Find out what you can do to prevent Didymo and invasive weeds being taken from one waterway to the next.

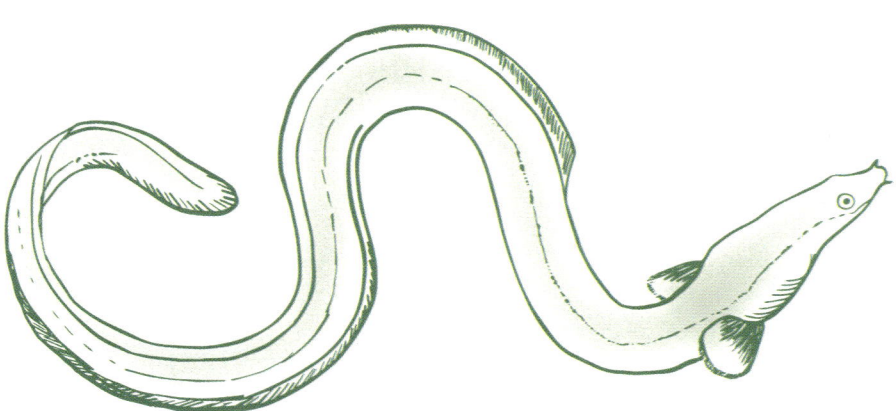

Nelson students investigating the health of their local waterways; planting native trees on river banks benefits the river and the creatures that live in it.

CATHERINE KIRBY

CLIMBING TREES FOR CONSERVATION

Growing up near Ōpōtiki in rural Bay of Plenty, Catherine Kirby was an explorer and tree climber. She and her friends would take off on their bikes to swim in the river, go to the beach or explore the bush.

'One of my favourite things was exploring places I hadn't been before. The bush had little waterfalls and big trees to swing from. I never had anyone teaching me the names of plants, but I was familiar with them. You get to know them even if you don't have a name for them.'

Catherine Kirby went to high school in Rotorua, an area surrounded by hot springs, boiling mud pools and geysers. Studying these and volcanoes at school got her hooked on earth sciences, which she went on to study at university. Catherine began to think about where she could make a positive difference and decided it was working to restore ecosystems such as forests. So she switched to botany and ecology, eventually becoming a specialist in native epiphytes: plants that perch up trees rather than grow on the ground. Her work in this area began when a fellow student also studying epiphytes needed someone to climb trees with her. 'Because that's what I spent my childhood doing, I couldn't wait to join her,' Catherine says.

Her studies in epiphytes also led her to write a book on the subject: *Field Guide to New Zealand's Epiphytes, Vines & Mistletoes*.

Catherine Kirby admits she has some hare-brained ideas at times, but she also has the passion and drive to make them happen. Her craziest idea so far was to create an image of a massive 40-metre-high rimu, showing the whole tree. Think of it like this: if you stand at the bottom of a tall tree and take a photo of it looking up, your image will show a very wide trunk with a tiny top disappearing into the sky. However, to show the rimu in proportion and the epiphytes in detail, the team needed to take photos of each section face-on and then 'stitch' them together. The resulting photo is part of the New Zealand Tree Project exhibition, travelling around galleries and museums in New Zealand.

It took 65 photos 'stitched' together to create the final portrait of the tree from Pureora Forest. The team photographing the giant rimu all brought different skills. Professional climbers used arborists' equipment to help the photographer instal a cable camera that can take photographs at different levels. The epiphyte ecologists, including Catherine Kirby, made decisions about the tree and what plants to be photographed.

EXPLORING THE WORLD OF EPIPHYTES & VINES

Studying epiphytes is a bit like exploring an unknown world. Because they live high up in the forest canopy, they are hard to see and so we know very little about them.

In the canopy, plants get a lot of sun. Sometimes, however, they are drenched with rain, but then they dry out again really quickly, so they have to have strategies to survive this dry-wet-dry-wet world.

Catherine Kirby studied how puka survives. Puka has very large leaves and grows into a small shrub or tree in the canopy. It starts off from a seed dropped by a bird into the canopy, and as it grows it also sends a root all the way to the ground so it can get additional water and nutrients from the earth at the base of the tree. It doesn't take over the tree.

Catherine and her colleagues also set up cameras to film what animals live in nest epiphytes. Nest epiphytes are clumps of plants in the tree that look like birds' nests. They found an amazing diversity of spiders and insects, as well as a gecko. Scientists have also found frogs living in nest epiphytes, and nesting birds such as kārearea/New Zealand falcon. Insects pollinate the flowers of nest epiphytes and birds and bats eat the fruit. But more research needs to be done to understand how important epiphytes are for animals.

The overlapping leaves of a nest epiphyte help trap water at the base of the plant, and also vegetation that will decompose and turn into soil. This means more epiphytes can join the nest epiphyte, so ferns or orchids might hang from them or shrub epiphytes grow out of them.

Top: Many of New Zealand's native forests have layers. Beginning at the forest floor, there is the understorey, the sub-canopy, the canopy and finally poking above, emergent trees. Here Catherine Kirby is studying an epiphyte nest in the canopy of a rimu tree. Below: A puka root descending from a tree to the forest floor.

WHAT IS AN EPIPHYTE?

Epiphytes are plants that grow on trees rather than on the ground. In the forest there is a lot of competition for sunlight, and epiphytes have solved the problem of how to get access to the sun by starting life high up in the canopy. They usually grow from a seed that a bird drops, which lands in the fork of a tree.

Ferns have spores rather than seeds. The spores are in little clusters (*sporangia*) on the backs of fronds. They are usually spread by wind. You can try growing ferns from spores by placing the *sporangia* on wet tissue paper. Keep the paper wet and make sure it is kept somewhere light but not too warm.

Many dry seeds are gathered easily from trees and plants in winter. Above: Dry seedpods in a patch of harakeke. Below: Some of the seeds we used for our seed bombs.

The first epiphytes to grow on a tree are usually ferns and mosses. As the tree grows taller and more branches grow, there are more places for epiphytes to take hold. The bigger the tree the better, which is why preserving big old trees in the forest is so important. A 26-metre-tall kahikatea tree in the South Island with a trunk 1.45 metres wide was found to have 28 different plant species growing on it.

Other plants that rely on trees are vines and mistletoe. Mistletoes put their roots into their host tree to tap into its sap. Vines get water and nutrients from their roots in the soil, but they use trees to hold on to as they make their way up to the sunlight at the top of the forest canopy.

carex seeds

TAKING ACTION: MAKING SEED BOMBS

In the forest, the seeds of many plants are spread by native birds. These include the seeds of epiphytes such as puka, as well as the seeds of trees such as tawa and karamu. But a challenge for trying to restore bush is that there may not be enough of the right birds to spread seeds.

Large seeds are spread by kererū, and smaller seeds are spread by korimako/bellbird, tūī and tauhou/silvereye.

One way to help forest restoration is to make seed bombs and then be a 'human bird', throwing the seed bombs (also called seed balls) into difficult-to-reach or gorse-covered areas.

harakeke seeds

kōwhai seeds

ACTIVITY

MAKING SEED BOMBS

In spring and summer, collect ripe berries and seed pods from native trees and plants, as close as possible to the area where the seed bombs will be thrown. Put them in labelled paper bags. At home, clean the seeds, removing the flesh from berries, dry the seeds and leave somewhere cool, dark and dry. Different berries will ripen at different times so it's important to collect over several months. You can also have a browse in winter to see which native plants have dried seedpods on them. It's best to make your seed bombs in autumn or winter when the seeds are fully dried.

You will need:

- ☆ newspaper
- ☆ seeds mixed together
- ☆ potting mix
- ☆ potter's clay without added chemicals
- ☆ gardening gloves

1. Lay out newspaper and place the potting mix and your seeds on it.
2. Take a piece of clay and flatten it into a disc about 15 centimetres in diameter. Place some potting mix in the middle and some of your seeds. Roll up into a ball, sealing the clay around the potting mix and seeds.
3. Leave the seed bombs somewhere dry and cool.
4. In winter, throw your seed bombs into areas difficult to access. An old tennis racket might help to send them even further.

WANT TO DO MORE?

If you live near mature forests, you can contribute to knowledge about epiphytes by taking part in a survey on the New Zealand Epiphyte Network website. Invasive weeds, such as old man's beard, are a big threat to our native forests. You can be a weed-buster and help protect our forests (see page 61).

NICOLA TOKI

THREATENED SPECIES AMBASSADOR

It's not surprising that Nicola Toki was a kid with a passion for nature. Her parents took her and her brother camping and fishing, and her nana could call fantails almost down to her finger. Nicola remembers bringing home all sorts of interesting finds as a child, from birds' nests and caterpillars to a dried shark's head. Part of her childhood was spent at Mount Cook Village in Aoraki Mount Cook National Park. She especially loved being around kea but learnt the hard way not to leave her bike outdoors overnight, as a kea ripped the seat to shreds.

At high school she helped start an environmental group called the 'Blue Planet Club', doing beach clean-ups and other activities. She won a 'Greengager' award when she was 16 for her environmental efforts. And she joined Project Jonah and learnt how to be an emergency marine mammal medic.

All these experiences while growing up in the shadow of Aoraki Mt Cook, with the bush and birds, the geckos and the invertebrates right on her doorstep motivated Nicola Toki to follow a career in conservation. 'I have a deep love for New Zealand's natural world. I wanted to spend my life encouraging others to care for our native wildlife as much as I do.' First, she studied zoology at university, undertaking a study of Adélie penguins. After this, she studied natural history filmmaking and communication, getting a job in an ecotourism company as a Hector's dolphins swimming guide. Now she is with the Department of Conservation as a media and public awareness officer.

A career highlight for Nicola was researching, writing and presenting over 200 episodes of 'Meet the Locals', a television series put together by DOC and TVNZ. It took her all around New Zealand telling the stories of our wildlife, wild places and people who protect them. She's also written books for children and has a popular regular radio slot called 'Critter of the Week' on RNZ, which highlights lesser-known threatened species.

As the threatened species ambassador for the Department of Conservation, Nicola Toki gets to meet a huge range of native species, including the kākāpō, kiwi, tuatara, and takahē. A favourite experience was getting up close to New Zealand's short-tailed bat for the first time. She was helping to catch the bats in the middle of the night to put tiny transmitters on their backs, when one crawled up her arm and climbed onto her head.

'The best part of being the threatened species ambassador is meeting the awesome people who work hard to protect our native wildlife, whether that's other DOC rangers, scientists, local iwi, communities or businesses. I also get to meet some very special wildlife.'

NICOLA TOKI

CARING FOR LIZARDS

New Zealand is sometimes known as the 'land of birds' but Nicola Toki says it should really be called the 'land of lizards'. New Zealand's native lizards are either geckos or skinks and there are thought to be more than 110 native species. They would once have been found in all our different habitats; but introduced predators and loss of habitat have had a big effect on native lizard populations.

Some lizards live in extreme environments, such as shingle slopes on mountains; some are nocturnal; some are well camouflaged. All of these factors make it hard to know just how many species there are and how large the population of each species is.

What we do know is that our lizard species are very diverse. Some are active during the day (diurnal), some at night (nocturnal), whereas others are active at dawn and at dusk (crepuscular). It can be hard to tell different species apart – scientists have only recently realised that what was called the common gecko is in fact several different species. Native geckos and almost all native skinks give birth to live young, which is very unusual, as in other countries most geckos and skinks lay eggs.

Unfortunately, being rare or unusual also makes lizards desirable to collectors (people who want to own rare lizards and keep them in captivity). Some collectors have tried to steal lizards and smuggle them out of the country. Customs agents do their best to catch people who try to do this. But once a lizard has been taken from its habitat by a smuggler, putting it back can be a risk, as scientists might not know exactly what habitat to return it to, or the lizard might have picked up a disease, which then wild lizards might catch. So smuggled lizards that have been rescued need to be cared for in captivity.

Nicola Toki has a permit to look after lizards, and she cares for several Northland green geckos and Canterbury geckos that were being smuggled. She says, 'It's harder than you might think to look after lizards. They eat live insects, so I'm forever trying to catch flies. Luckily my husband is a black-belt in martial arts, with lightening reflexes, so he catches them in his hands! They also need to have the right plants in their enclosure, and to be kept at the right humidity and temperature. New Zealand geckos are very unusual in that they can live for decades, compared with other geckos that only live for two or three years, so I'll be looking after these for my whole life.'

The best place for a lizard is to be living wild in its natural habitat, therefore scientists and conservation groups are trying to find ways to protect lizard species by using predator control, building fences, or moving lizards to suitable safe habitats.

The tuatara is not a lizard, but just like lizards they are reptiles. They once were an endangered species, but because of successful conservation management, their numbers are increasing.

THREATENED SPECIES FACTS

In the 750 years since humans arrived, at least 76 bird species, three frogs, at least three lizards, one freshwater fish, four plants and an unknown number of invertebrate species have become extinct. Of 13,000 species of plants and animals that were assessed by DOC for a threatened species strategy:

- more than 3000 are classified as threatened or at risk, with around 800 classified as at risk of extinction
- another 3000 species can't be classified as we don't know enough yet to know whether they are threatened

TAKING ACTION: CREATE A LIZARD HABITAT IN YOUR GARDEN

Lizards can live happily in gardens, school grounds and reserves if they have the right kind of habitat and protection. Untidy gardens with lots of places to hide and keep safe are great for lizards. Rock piles, dead wood, and dense ground-cover plants are all good hiding places. Sunny places where they can keep warm and bask in the sun are also important for them.

Lizards eat insects as well as berries and nectar. Insects do well in gardens with plenty of mulch. Plants that have berries include coprosmas and kawakawa. Plants with nectar include flax and mānuka. A garden that is good for lizards will also be good for native birds, so even if you don't see lizards straight away you might see more birds around the garden.

〜〜〜

ACTIVITY

MAKING A LIZARD HOME

You will need:

- ☆ rocks or untreated wood
- ☆ native plants
- ☆ optional: Unduline – a manufactured roofing material (see step 6)

1. Visit the DOC website to find out what kind of lizards you might have in your or your neighbours' gardens. Find out about the lizards: What do they eat? Do they like basking in the sun? Are they nocturnal?
2. Now survey your garden looking for suitable lizard habitats. Draw up a plan of your garden and mark on it sunny spots, rock piles, plant cover and other suitable hiding places and plant food sources.
3. If you find some suitable habitats or food, extend these areas with more plant cover or by adding rock or wood piles. Think about how the lizards might move around from the ground into trees or from one area to another. Is the habitat linked to trees or to other areas by vines?
4. If your garden doesn't yet have a suitable habitat, draw up a plan.
5. Set up predator traps to keep as many lizard predators out of the area as possible. Make sure the cover can keep them safe from cats.
6. If you have Unduline, try creating a lizard home by stacking small squares of it.

WANT TO DO MORE?

There are many things you can do to create and protect lizard habitats. For example, you can join a local conservation project and find out what they are doing and how you can help. Find out about the plague skink, an unwanted Australian skink that is in some parts of the North Island.

Opposite top: These lizard gardens include hand-painted signs to remind people not to walk through or disturb the area.
Opposite below: An elegant gecko in a flowering mānuka.

LIZARD PERMITS

Native lizards are protected by wildlife laws. People need a permit from the Department of Conservation to hold them in captivity. Even handling lizards requires a permit. These laws are designed to protect lizards, and the permit system means that lizards are cared for by people who have the skills and equipment to look after them properly.

TIPS FOR SPOTTING LIZARDS

- Use binoculars to look for skinks on rocks or bushes, stay still and see if you can spot them basking in the sun.
- Use a torch to spotlight at night for a nocturnal gecko. Look for their eyes reflecting the torch light.

- Leave lizards alone, only picking them up if you need to rescue them from a cat, for example. Lizards get stressed very easily and may drop their tail, which reduces their chances of survival.

TIP

If you have tracking tunnels set up (page 12), look out for lizard footprints. Gecko (left) and skink prints look something like this:

ANTHONY BEHRENS

WEED-BUSTER & WHIO PROTECTOR

Along with his partner, Fiona, Anthony Behrens has undertaken some epic adventures in New Zealand's wild places. A few years back they spent three months tramping from one end of the South Island to the other on the Te Araroa Trail. More recently they walked from Wellington to Coromandel on a trail they called the Spine of the Fish, which Anthony describes as their biggest and best adventure. Tramping the Spine of the Fish through rugged mountains and along backcountry roads took them 62 days.

Anthony Behrens is a designer and photographer and his partner Fiona is a radiographer. They only took up tramping about 10 years ago but that led to their first volunteer project with the Ruahine Whio Protectors. 'On one of our first tramps in the Ruahine Ranges we followed a stoat trapline up a mountain. Four of the traps contained dead stoats – we'd never seen stoats before. We rang the Department of Conservation to tell them about the stoats and they put us in touch with the Ruahine Whio Protectors.' They joined the protectors and now help service some of the 3000 traps in the rugged Ruahine Ranges.

While returning from one of the Ruahine Whio Protector trips, Anthony noticed wild pine seedlings popping up in an area where pines had been felled. The area was being left to return to native forest, but Anthony could see that this wouldn't happen if the pines were left to grow. He and Fiona started pulling out the seedlings. This was the beginning of the Palmy Pine Pulling Posse in the Ruahine Ranges. The 'posse', a small group of volunteers, has removed more than 7000 wilding pines. Anthony and Fiona were excited to discover fernbirds living in the area. They'd never seen fernbirds before and it seems no one else had, either. They've even named the area Fernbird Gully.

Their tramping adventures have totally changed the way Anthony looks at nature. Walking though the Coromandel and seeing the kauri dieback problem and how little was being done has made him very concerned for the future of native ecosystems. At times, too, the wilding pines removal seems almost an impossible task – as quickly as one area is cleared, pines are growing out of control in other places.

'It is hard work pulling pines but weirdly satisfying because the impact of what we're doing is instant.'

ANTHONY BEHRENS

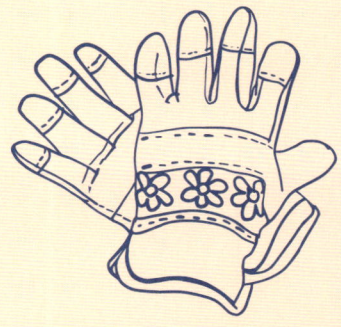

Mātātā/fernbirds are declining in numbers. They are very secretive and poor fliers so are rarely seen.

However, long-distance hiking has taught them both the value of perseverance. 'Our favourite motto while out walking, trapping or pulling pines is, "How do you eat an elephant? One bite at a time." The basic idea is that every dead wilding pine is a good thing. One dead seedling is better than a mature pine.' And there is satisfaction to be had from the job of clearing pines. 'Weed-busting is conservation work where you can see the results straight away. You can look back and see the good you've done.'

WILDING PINES & OTHER WEEDS

Weeds are often described as 'a plant in the wrong place'. In some of New Zealand's natural habitats such as wetlands, native forests, tussock grasslands, lakes and streams, there are many weeds. These weeds are introduced plants that have spread into wild places, often from people's gardens. When they spread into native habitats, some become pest plants and do harm by altering and damaging the habitat, for example, the old man's beard vine smothers native forests and kills trees; lupins take over a river bed, making it hard for birds to find places to nest; and wandering willie covers the ground and prevents young native plants from growing.

Gorse is a well-known example of an introduced plant becoming a weed. Gorse is used in Scotland and northern England as hedges, but in New Zealand's warmer climate, gorse grows more quickly, and the hedges people planted here long ago soon spread to cover whole hillsides, taking over farmland that once had been native forest.

Trees can also be weeds. Introduced conifers do damage when they grow in the wrong place. Conifers are trees that have cones, such as pine and fir trees, and are often planted in large plantations to provide wood for construction. But because their seeds are carried by the wind they can 'escape' these

PROTECTING REMOTE WILD PLACES

The area where the Palmy Pine Pulling Posse are working to clear wilding pines is a two-hour drive from Palmerston North. That's a lot of petrol and a lot of time on the road just to get there and back. Many of the traps the Ruahine Whio Protectors monitor are even more remote and require hours of tramping through rugged country. Some traps can't be reached when it snows or floods and others require a helicopter to get to them. These conditions make it both expensive and difficult to protect our wild places.

Whio/blue ducks are at risk of extinction. They live in backcountry rivers. Stoats are the greatest danger, as they will attack females on their nests, steal eggs and take young ducklings.

Anthony's partner, Fiona, ready to spring into action with her weed-busting tools.

plantations and end up taking over native landscapes. When they do this, they are called wilding conifers or wilding pines.

Wilding pines are thirsty. When they take over from tussock grasslands or other areas where there was no forest, they need much more water than the original grasslands do. This means there is less water in streams and rivers and this has a big effect on farms and towns that rely on this water.

Conifers, including pines, drop their needles on the ground around them. These needles make the soil around the trees acidic. Other trees and plants won't grow in this acidic soil, which is why a pine forest is usually a one-species forest. Pine forests don't have the same food for native birds and insects that a forest of native trees supplies, so while some animals are able to live in pine forests, they aren't the best habitat for our native species.

TAKING ACTION: GETTING RID OF PEST PLANTS

Being a weed-buster can be really rewarding because you can see the results straight away. However, as some weeds can be difficult to get rid of and may grow back, you will need perseverance to ensure your hard work pays off. The Weedbusters website, www.weedbusters.org.nz, recommends starting small, and working in stages, replanting the area with native plants as you go. If the job is too big for you, drawing up a weed map and sharing it is a good first step to making people aware of the problem.

HOW PLANTS SPREAD

Most plants spread through seeds that are either wind-blown, such as the seeds of conifers, or carried by birds, such as the seeds of Darwin's barberry.

Conifers grow seeds within their cones, and when the cones are ripe, they open and the seeds are blown by the wind. Darwin's barberry seeds are inside a berry. The bird eats the berry and then excretes the seed out.

Some plants can also grow from pieces of the plant being moved. Plants like tradescantia (wandering willie) can grow from a single broken-off piece of the plant. Others like wild ginger can spread under the ground using rhizomes, which then grow into new plants.

ACTIVITY
WEED-BUSTING

What weeds are a problem in your area? You may know where you want to do some weed-busting already, but if not, find out what weeds are causing a problem in your area. There are so many different plants it can be hard to work out which are pests and which are not. Here are some useful tools to help you:

✪ Weedbusters has *Plant me Instead* booklets for each region. These describe the worst weeds in the region. They also show what plants people could plant in their gardens instead.

✪ Use iNaturalist to identify plants by posting photographs. If the plant is on the National Pest Plant Accord list, this will come up on its iNaturalist page: naturalist.nz/home

✪ See Resources and Further Information page 75 for more tools.

WEED-BUSTING IDEAS

1. Draw up a weed map showing where the worst pest plants are in and around your school grounds or local community. You could share this with your class, your local residents' association or council.

2. Talk to the right people. If the weeds you've found are around your house or property, talk to your family and get them on board with your plan. If the weeds are in a public area, get in touch with your local council, regional council or other organisation responsible for that area. There may already be a group working there you can join, or the council might help you get started. Some councils provide native plants that can be planted in the cleared area.

3. Get rid of the weeds you have found. Look up your weeds on the Weedbusters site. Some plants can be left to rot on the ground where you pull them up, others will have to be taken to your local tip or refuse transfer station. You will need to enlist some adults to help if the weeds need spraying or to be taken to the tip.

4. What will happen to the area once you've removed the weeds? The Palmy Pine Pulling Posse are working in an area where the native plants are already regenerating, but it's likely that in an urban area the space will fill up with new weeds unless you plant native plants.

5. It's a good idea to have gardening gloves and hi-vis vests, while the rest of the equipment will depend on the kind of weeds you are removing, for example, secateurs, loppers, gardening forks, bags to collect weed material for the tip.

WANT TO DO MORE?

Find a way to educate people about the problem of garden plants escaping and becoming pest plants. As an example, Anthony Behrens created a YouTube video called 'Fernbird Gully' about the Palmy Pine Pulling Posse.

CAN GORSE BE GOOD?

Sometimes, gorse can work as a nursery for native plants, protecting seedlings from animals such as sheep or goats. Once the native plants grow through the gorse and shade it from light, the gorse dies off. Therefore, in some cases, gorse could be left to eventually regenerate into native bush. This only works if there are native seeds being dropped by birds, which then take root and grow through the gorse.

Illustration of gorse, New Zealand's most widely recognised weed, by Otto Wilhelm Thomé (1885). Gorse was introduced to New Zealand around that time and was meant to be an ornamental hedge before it spread so widely that it became a problem.

JORDAN ARIA HOUSIAUX

MARINE SCIENTIST

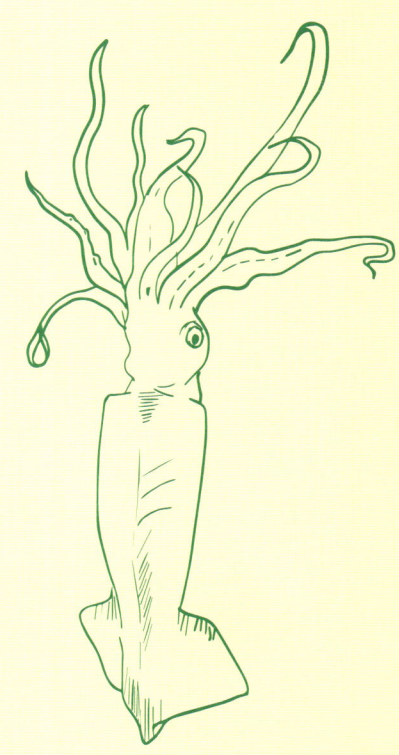

Jordan Aria Housiaux is of Te Ātiawa ki Whakarongotai, Ngāti Toa, and Ngāti Raukawa descent.

Brought up at the beach and by rivers, she was a real water baby, with fond memories of a childhood spent paddling, surfing and swimming. Her parents played canoe polo, were involved in the surf club, and enjoyed fishing and kayaking. Jordan played canoe polo too, captaining the Paddle Ferns and leading them to victory at the World Championships in 2016.

Anyone that spends this much time at the beach is sure to see dolphins and whales, and those moments stand out in Jordan's memories of her childhood. And then when she chose to study marine biology at university, her obsession with sharks began. 'I love that they are these huge animals, but they move so gracefully through the water and can travel really long distances. I think sharks can be quite misunderstood, as people find them scary. But sharks really are beautiful, amazing animals.'

While she was studying at Otago University, she also worked part-time at the Marine Studies Centre. She worked as an educator with rangatahi on marine-science days and camps. The students were able to work on their own marine science projects, planning, carrying out and presenting their results. Jordan Aria Housiaux enjoyed seeing the students learn to take charge of their own learning. Most of their projects were centred around the sharks held in the tanks at the Marine Studies Centre.

Now that her own shark study is complete (next page) Jordan is studying pilot whales. Again, she is in awe of these animals. She's hoping to find out more about pilot whale strandings and what might help them survive a stranding. Jordan plans to use both indigenous Māori knowledge as well as Western science in her work. 'We are often taught that Western science is the only way to study things. But indigenous cultures have for many generations used and developed their own unique knowledge systems and methods to answer questions and thrive in the world around them.'

'Being a scientist is all about asking questions and doing experiments to figure out the answers. The cool thing about being a marine scientist is we get to do our experiments in the ocean.'

JORDAN ARIA HOUSIAUX

UNDERSTANDING SHARKS

Broadnosed sevengill sharks are important apex predators of coastal regions around the world. They eat a wide range of fish, octopus and other marine species. Sevengill sharks are found around New Zealand, but not much was known about them and they became the subject of Jordan Aria Housiaux's research for her Masters in science.

There are a range of study techniques that shark scientists can use. Jordan explains that after researching what she wished to find out, 'You head out on a boat and attract sharks using chum (lots of fishy smelly bits) and depending on what questions you are trying to answer, you put tags on the sharks that you attract.'

After a period of time, these tags detach from the shark and float up to the surface and they can be found using GPS technology. The tags record how deep the sharks swam, how warm the water was, where the sharks swam to, and so on. Shark scientists also take small skin scrapes from the fin of the shark, and analyse the samples in the lab to look at their DNA. This can supply information such as whether sharks in different places are related to one another.

Jordan, with the help of her team, did over 70 survey trips to gather data. They recorded measurements such as water temperature, cloud cover and sea conditions, and then compared this to the number of sevengill sharks they counted. As well as tagging sharks, they took photos of the individual sharks. The photographs taken during this research show that sevengill sharks have unique spots all over them, which can be used to identify individuals, just like fingerprints in humans or markings on orca.

BROADNOSED SEVENGILL SHARK FACTS

- They can grow up to 3 metres long.
- Females are generally larger than males.
- They weigh up to 100 kilograms.
- They have seven gills – most other sharks have five.
- Sometimes they hunt together to take large prey.
- They are sometimes eaten by great white sharks and orca.

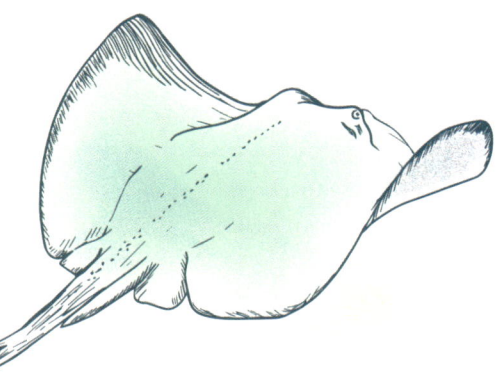

She discovered that most of the year, sevengill sharks can be found in Paterson Inlet on Stewart Island/Rakiura, as well as Otago Harbour in Dunedin. But in winter, fewer were found in Paterson Inlet, and none at all in Otago Harbour. It seems these sharks like to be where the water is warmer. She thinks this is because there's more prey to eat when the water temperature is higher.

Understanding when the sharks are present in these harbours is helpful to ensure the species' survival. For example, to protect the sharks, it might be necessary to consider a marine reserve or to have different rules about when and where people can fish.

TAKING ACTION: KAITIAKI OF OUR OCEANS

Ask Jordan Aria Housiaux about the role kaitiaki can play in caring for our oceans and she suggests spending time at the beach with your friends and family, having fun swimming between the flags and catching waves, and learning about what lives there by doing the marine metre-squared activity (page 28) are all great ways. 'The more we enjoy and respect our marine spaces, the more likely we are to look after them,' she says.

Taking action to reduce our plastic waste and keep our oceans clean are some of the best things we can do to protect the marine space.

THE ROLE OF SHARKS IN THE ECOSYSTEM

'We need people to start seeing and understanding sharks as an asset to our oceans. They really help the whole ecosystem stay healthy and diverse,' says Jordan. She explains how sharks are at the top of the food web in the ocean, but if the number of sharks keeps declining, it will also cause a huge disturbance to other beautiful creatures found in the ocean.

'Pollution that impacts our marine environment is a huge problem. This can be plastics going out to sea, or in the form of greenhouse gases in the atmosphere causing our oceans to warm.'

JORDAN ARIA HOUSIAUX

BEACH CLEAN-UP & LITTER-MONITORING

A dead gannet, with plastic fishing net tangled in its beak.

You will need:

- ☆ bags for the rubbish
- ☆ gloves
- ☆ spades
- ☆ sun protection, first-aid kit

1. Plan ahead. Get support for your clean-up from the local council or DOC office and/or Sustainable Coastlines.
2. Do your clean-up at low tide.
3. Encourage others from your school, Scouts, Guides or other groups to become involved.
4. Work out how you will dispose of the rubbish you find – perhaps a parent can take it to the local tip or the council might agree to pick it up.
5. Make sure you and the other participants think about health and safety. Be prepared to deal with sharp objects such as broken glass. Make sure everyone is being sun smart. Be aware of the tides.

TAKE YOUR CLEAN-UP A STEP FURTHER

Pay attention to where the most waste has gathered. What do you think has caused this? It might be the water currents, wave action or a storm. Now you know this is the area you might need to come back regularly.

Do a survey of the waste you've found. What were the most frequently found objects? Is there something you can do about this? For example, can you work out where these objects are coming from? Can you contact the manufacturers and urge them to manage waste better? Or is this something the community could do something about?

For example, students involved in Project Hotspot Taranaki surveyed the rubbish they found. They kept finding strange plastic-fringed objects, which they identified as shotgun wads from gun cartridges. A bit of detective work and help from their teacher and some scientists and they discovered these were coming from a shooting club near a river. It didn't take much to persuade the clay pigeon shooting club to switch to biodegradable wads.

WANT TO DO MORE?

Get involved in the Sustainable Coastlines citizen science project to monitor and gather data about litter around New Zealand's beaches.

'Beach clean-ups are a good way to see how much pollution we are really putting into our marine space. Take a group of friends and pick up all the different bits of rubbish and plastic you find The ocean animals will thank you for it.'

JORDAN ARIA HOUSIAUX

RANGATAHI
YOUTH NATURE HEROES

BRANDON INTERMEDIATE SCHOOL
ENVIRO TEAM
FRESHWATER GUARDIANS

Porirua's Brandon Intermediate Enviro Team are working to make Cannons Creek Lake, and the streams that connect the lake to the sea, a healthier and better place for fish to live. They've installed fish ladders and baffles, which are structures designed to make it easier for fish to get around dams and over barriers and move freely up and down a waterway.

Around the streams, new plants are starting to shade the water and make it a better habitat for native fish. An eel came to inspect the work of the Enviro Team while they were installing baffles in a stream and they took this as a good sign that their work is starting to pay off.

The team, Marley Fretton, Mayala Parau, Jak Ruatapu, Israel Ah-Hoi Mihaka, Aaron Moe and Ezra Crawshaw, are determined to do their bit to save native fish species and keep the streams clean. Three of them, Marley, Mayala and Jak, started work with Mountains to Sea Wellington (see page 71) on this kaitiakitanga project in 2017. They were amazed to find that what they called the 'duck pond' is actually named Cannons Creek Lake. Marley says, 'People used to swim and kayak in it. There are even stories of our school going there, back in the olden days, and training for kayaking championships.' Today, a kayak would get stuck in the silt.

The team first surveyed the river to find out what was living there. Then they put together a plan of action with the help of Mountains to Sea Wellington and Partners Porirua. They presented to their local council, applying for 'Make it Happen' grants to pay for fish experts to help with the fish ladders and baffles, as well as for trees to plant along the river bank. Meeting Mayor Mike Tana and the council was a highlight of the project. The boys were surprised how interested the council were in their proposal, and this interest helped motivate the boys even more. Once the Enviro Team received funding, they went to the council nursery to choose trees to plant and fish experts helped them put in the fish ladders and baffles. The baffles slow the water flow, making it easier for fish to swim upstream. The boys tested how the baffles worked using ping-pong balls as fish.

It's up to Ezra and Aaron to keep the project going now, as Marley, Mayala, Jak and Israel are off to college. Their advice to Ezra, Aaron, and others around New Zealand is, 'Just get out there, don't be afraid to get your hands dirty. You'll be benefitting the next generation.'

'Just get out there, don't be afraid to get your hands dirty. You'll be benefitting the next generation.'

BRANDON INTERMEDIATE ENVIRO TEAM

The Brandon Intermediate Enviro Team putting fish ladders and baffles into the streams below Cannons Creek Lake.

GEORGE HOBSON
CARING FOR BIRDS

George Hobson has been running the Bird of the Year campaign for the pohowera/banded dotterel since he was 12 years old. 'It was about two weeks before Bird of the Year 2015 and I'd seen my first pohowera just a week before – they are absolutely adorable. I checked out the Bird of the Year website and to my surprise there was no one running their campaign. In fact, they weren't even featured on the website. I quickly emailed Forest & Bird head office asking if the pohowera could be added to the competition and they agreed!' From small beginnings, the campaign has built up followers, and in 2018 the pohowera received more than 1000 votes.

Running the campaign isn't the only thing George Hobson does for the pohowera. He's also involved in a pohowera/banded dotterel nesting study on Wellington Harbour's eastern shore, which aims to find out more about how to protect the birds while they are nesting on the beach.

George Hobson's interest in birds started when he was 10. He was looking after someone's pet cockatiels and discovered he had a talent for working with birds. Being home-schooled made it easy for him to take this passion further. He became a Zealandia youth ambassador, learning about the sanctuary's work and spending time engaging with school groups and other young people who visit the sanctuary. George also helped set up a national group called Young Birders New Zealand. And at just 16, he's already won plenty of awards for his work, including the 2018 Forest & Bird Youth Award.

Young Birders New Zealand fills a gap in environmental groups for teenagers and young people. The team all live in different parts of New Zealand and communicate with each other via group chats, social media, and they produce a bi-monthly online magazine, *Fledgling*. Through the group, members get access to amazing field trips organised by Birds New Zealand. 'I love communicating with our members. It's really wonderful to talk to these amazing young people, who are clearly the enviro-leaders of the future. We're really lucky at YBNZ. We have incredible people with a wide range of ages and skill levels.'

George's advice to other young people who want to get involved in conservation is, 'Do it. The world needs you.' He admits there are challenges. 'The natural earth needs all the help it can get, and we as rangatahi need to rise to the challenge. The challenge of introduced predators, the challenge of climate change, even the challenge of recycling. We need to be using our collective youth voice to make positive change for the world. You *can* make a difference.'

Top: George Hobson holding a black petrel.
Above: A banded dotterel.

RILEY HATHAWAY
OCEAN ADVOCATE

Riley Hathaway and Steve, her underwater cameraman dad, have been shooting videos about life in the ocean since Riley was 13. At the time of writing this book, they'd made 20 five-minute episodes for television and their Young Ocean Explorers website has hours of video, polls, quizzes and lots more. They've also published a children's book, *Love our Ocean*, and they visit schools around the country to encourage children to care for the ocean.

Young Ocean Explorers began as a school project. Riley asked her dad to help her make a video about how turtles are endangered by plastic rubbish, which included Riley interviewing a turtle expert. Steve saw how other children responded to the video as well as seeing first-hand Riley's passion for the marine world. The idea behind the first videos was born.

Young Ocean Explorers aims to inspire kids to love our ocean, through entertaining education. 'We want to capture children's imaginations through great storytelling, and bring the beauty, awe and fascination of the ocean and its inhabitants alive.'

It's not surprising that much of the message behind Young Ocean Explorers is showing kids how they can care for marine life. 'Imagine if we each picked up one piece of plastic rubbish a day from our local environment,' says Riley, 'what a difference that would make.'

Filming Young Ocean Explorers has given Riley some great opportunities. A highlight was a trip to Palau in the western Pacific Ocean, where she did her first SCUBA dive. 'I saw five different manta rays, which was insane. They are big, friendly, beautiful giants and so graceful underwater.' Riley looks and sounds confident in the videos, but it hasn't always been that way. Like many people she was influenced by movies and negative stories about sharks, making her nervous about encountering them. As she worked on the series it helped her understand them better and she's even swum with sharks near the Kermadec Islands.

Above: The cover of *Love our Ocean*, by Steve and Riley Hathaway.
Below: Riley, with her dad Steve.

Fitting in school work has sometimes been pretty difficult, but Riley's school has been supportive of her ocean advocacy work. This work also led her to present to 2500 people at a TEDx Auckland event. 'Doing all this with Young Ocean Explorers is like taking an actual school subject, I've learnt and am still continuously learning so much. I love it!' Now 18, Riley has finished school, and she hopes to have more time for researching stories and writing scripts.

For young people wanting to advocate for nature, Riley says, 'My advice would be to just pick up a camera and start filming. Practice makes perfect and with technology and social media nowadays, anything is possible.'

Left: Devante Nichols, Ryan Tinney, and Carter Birmingham presenting to the Porirua community about their pest-free programme.

'The natural earth needs all the help it can get, and we as rangatahi need to rise to the challenge. The challenge of introduced predators, the challenge of climate change, even the challenge of recycling.'

GEORGE HOBSON

TAKING ACTION: SPEAKING UP FOR NATURE

The Enviro Team from Brandon Intermediate School, George Hobson and Riley Hathaway are all speaking up for nature in different ways. They are communicating and passing on their passion for nature, rivers, birds and the ocean with other young people and with adults. They are encouraging others to take action, whether that's picking up plastic on the beach, keeping dogs on leads to protect nesting birds, or supporting a stream restoration.

ACTIVITY

SPEAKING UP FOR NATURE

Below: Riley Hathaway reporting for Young Ocean Explorers.

There are many ways to speak up and take a stand for nature, from being a role model to running a campaign.

PERSONAL ACTIONS: BEING A ROLE MODEL

By acting the way you would like others to behave, you are being a role model and your actions can encourage others to do the same. For example, picking up rubbish, joining a tree-planting day, riding your bike instead of asking to be driven to sport practice, carrying re-useable drink bottles and cloth shopping bags – all these ways and more show people around you what you stand for.

INFLUENCING WHĀNAU AND CLOSE FRIENDS

The people you are most likely to influence are your friends and whānau. You could encourage your group of friends to start riding bikes to school and have litter-free lunches. Think about doing some of the projects in this book with your

friends and family, such as Leave No Trace, the Garden Bird Survey and Creating a Lizard Habitat in your garden. You could also find out about local projects and encourage them to take part.

COMMUNICATING WITH OTHERS IN YOUR SCHOOL AND LOCAL COMMUNITY

Your next steps might be to spread your ideas further, maybe within your school through an assembly presentation, through a blog, or at a community event. It's a good idea to have data to help get your message across. For example, you could share the results of a beach clean-up survey, using photos and graphs, and bring along some of the rubbish you have collected to highlight your message, such as plastic straws. Spend some time thinking about how to reach your audience. Try to put yourself in their shoes: what do they care about? They might not know much about the animals that live in the harbour but they might care about being able to swim in clean water. Make your presentation memorable by using video or photos. You could do something fun such as hand out chocolate fish when you are talking about the plight of fish in the harbour.

INFLUENCING LOCAL AND NATIONAL GOVERNMENT

Maybe you want to influence the government to change rules or do more for nature? You could write letters or submissions to your local council, or local MP, even to the prime minister. Check who makes the rules about the particular issue you are concerned about and direct your letter to them. Be polite. Be creative. Can you use any of the ideas above to make your letter stand out?

'Imagine if we each picked up one piece of plastic rubbish a day from the environment, what a difference that would make.' **RILEY HATHAWAY**

TIPS

- It is much easier to encourage people to do things when you use positive messages. Find ways to use 'do' rather than 'don't'. For example, 'do take re-usable bags when you go shopping' is better than 'don't bring home more plastic bags'. It is also easier to encourage others to do things when they are fun, so if your friends say they'll come with you to pick up rubbish at the beach, promise to play a game with them afterwards or take a picnic.
- Keep your group safe. It's better to be a positive role model than getting angry with strangers you see littering.

- Set some rules about behaviour online; decide what is acceptable and stick with it. Get help from a trusted adult if you are bullied.
- Decide how much time you can commit to your project before you start. George and Riley both say their projects take lots of time. But they both say it's worth it.
- If you want to set up an interest group like Young Birders NZ, George Hobson's advice is: 'Go for it! It's an amazing experience setting up a group. It is important to have a team behind you – maybe that's a couple of friends or your siblings but it's really helpful to have some support.'

Taking part in conservation activities and education programmes such as Mountains to Sea Wellington are great opportunities to get outdoors and learn new skills.

EDUCATION PROGRAMMES

Find out what programmes are running in your area. Maybe your school could get involved. Mountains to Sea Wellington delivers education programmes to students across the Wellington region. They also support community groups, schools and partners with kaitiakitanga projects and citizen science.

BEING A NATURE HERO

Many of the heroes in this book started off with a small step – one wilding pine pulled out of the ground, a school project about turtles and rubbish, going to see an albatross at Taiaroa Head, placing a vote in the Bird of the Year competition.

If you've heard Nicola Toki on the radio, watched Riley Hathaway on video or visited George Hobson's Bird of the Year campaign page, you'll see how much fun and enjoyment they get out of working for nature.

I hope that the stories, activities and tips in this book give you ideas about some small steps you could take on your own journey to becoming a nature hero. Have fun along the way.

RESOURCES AND FURTHER INFORMATION

GENERAL

See www.discovernature.nz/nature-heroes for up-to-date resources and links.

Biographies and conservation stories
www.teara.govt.nz

New Zealand Geographic (magazine)
www.nzgeo.com

Forest and Bird (magazine)
www.forestandbird.org.nz/magazine

Volunteer groups
www.naturespace.org.nz/groups

Identification of plants and animals
www.inaturalist.nz/home

Safety outdoors
www.adventuresmart.nz

RICHARD HENRY

Habits of the Flightless Birds of New Zealand: with notes on other birds, Richard Henry, Government Print, 1903. It is available from the National Library of New Zealand.

Kākāpō
www.doc.govt.nz/kakapo-recovery

Tracking tunnels and chew cards
www.doc.govt.nz

www.landcareresearch.co.nz

Identifying footprints
www.pestdetective.org.nz/culprits

Chew card interpretation notes
landcareresearch.co.nz

Interpretation of animal tooth impressions
www.naturespace.org.nz

Build a trapping tunnel
www.doc.govt.nz/get-involved

PÉRRINE MONCRIEFF

Learning about birds
nzbirdsonline.org.nz

Bird identification online course
www.doc.govt.nz/get-involved

Bird counts
Garden Bird Survey
www.landcareresearch.co.nz

Great Kererū Count
www.greatkererucount.nz

National bird-banding scheme
www.birdsnz.org.nz/schemes/nz-national-banding-scheme

Recording bird sightings
ebird.org/newzealand/home

birdatlas.co.nz

Youth organisations
Young Birders
www.youngbirdersnz.com

Kiwi Conservation Club
kcc.org.nz

Forest and Bird Youth
www.forestandbird.org.nz

Birds NZ Youth Camps
www.birdsnz.org.nz/birding/bird-nz-youth-camps

LANCE RICHDALE

Seabird Genius: The Story of L.E. Richdale, The Royal Albatross and the Yellow-Eyed Penguin, Neville Peat, Otago University Press, 2011

Albatross and other seabirds
Royal Albatross Centre
albatross.org.nz

Yellow-eyed penguins
www.yellow-eyedpenguin.org.nz

Royal albatross cam
www.doc.govt.nz/royalcam

Old footage of Agnes Richdale and albatross
digitalnz.org/records/3682163O/royal-albatross-
and-chick-at-taiaroa-head-1939

Protecting shore and river birds
Ecological restoration groups in New Zealand
www.naturespace.org.nz/groups

Building nest boxes
www.doc.govt.nz/globalassets/documents/
conservation/native-animals/birds/nest-box-
design.pdf

blog.tepapa.govt.nz

Banded birds
www.doc.govt.nz/our-work/bird-banding

Wildlife rescue
WReNNZ Wildlife Rehabilitators Network
www.wrenz.or.nz

Bird rescue
www.nzbirds.com

BETTY BATHAM

Portobello Marine Research Station
Southern Seas: Discovering Marine Life at 46°South,
by John Jillet, Keith Probert, Sally Carson, University
of Otago Press, 2005

Marine metre squared project
www.mm2.net.nz

Identification guides
Free identification guides from
www.mm2.net.nz

Free App: NZ Marine Field Guide

DON MERTON

Don Merton, the man who saved the black robin
by Alison Ballance, Reed, 2007

*The Black Robin: Saving the world's most endangered
bird* by David Butler and Don Merton, OUP, 1993

Feeding garden birds
www.forestandbird.org.nz

Attract birds to your garden
www.doc.govt.nz

How to make a bird water-feeder
youtu.be/q6EitavSRNg

GEORGE GIBBS

New Zealand Wētā by George Gibbs, Reed, 1998

Article by George Gibbs
www.nzgeo.com/stories/the-demon-grasshoppers

Wētā online guide
wetageta.massey.ac.nz/index.html

Building wētā motels
www.doc.govt.nz

images.tvnz.co.nz/tvnz_images

www.friendsofhunuaranges.co.nz

www.sciencelearn.org.nz/images

Make a bug motel
www.gogardening.co.nz

INGRID VISSER

Swimming with Orca, Dr Ingrid N. Visser,
Penguin, 2006

Ingrid's Orca Research Trust
www.orcaresearch.org

Marine mammal strandings
Orca 0800 SEE ORCA (0800 733 6722)

DOC Hotline 0800 362 468

Project Jonah 0800 4 WHALE (0800 4 94253)

Whale rescue organisation
www.projectjonah.org.nz

NZ sighting sheet
www.orcaresearch.org

Free App: Hector's Dolphin sightings
(for all marine mammals)

Identifying whales at sea
www.environment.gov.au

Rules for behaviour around marine mammals
www.doc.govt.nz

MIRIAM RITCHIE

Miriam Ritchie and Woody on YouTube
www.youtube.com/watch?v=19NBYCdOl_U

Conservation Dogs programme
Partnership with Kiwibank
www.doc.govt.nz/about-us/our-partners
Conservation dogs programme
www.doc.govt.nz/our-work

Kiwi-avoidance training for dogs
www.kiwisforkiwi.org

Leave No Trace
www.leavenotrace.org.nz

Visiting pest-free islands
www.doc.govt.nz

Kauri dieback
www.kauridieback.co.nz

Didymo
www.mpi.govt.nz

PĀTAKA MOORE & CALEB ROYAL

Maori and the Environment: Kaitiaki,
Rachel Selby, Pātaka Moore,
Malcolm Mulholland, Huia Publishers, 2010

Local community projects
www.naturespace.org.nz

Freshwater and estuaries, ID guides
and fact sheets
www.niwa.co.nz/freshwater-and-estuaries

www.landcareresearch.co.nz

Water quality
LAWA (Land Air Water Aotearoa)
www.lawa.org.nz

Didymo
www.mpi.govt.nz/travel-and-recreation

Fish passage, fish ladders and fish
climbing upstream
www.doc.govt.nz/fishpassage
fishladdersolutions.co.nz

What shouldn't be in stormwater drains
www.wellingtonwater.co.nz/your-water
www.aucklandcouncil.govt.nz/environment

CATHERINE KIRBY

Field Guide to New Zealand's Epiphytes,
Vines & Mistletoes, Catherine Kirby,
University of Waikato, 2016

The New Zealand Tree Project
www.nztreeproject.com
www.nzgeo.com/stories/islands-in-the-sky

Collecting seeds for propagation
www.doc.govt.nz/get-involved
www.naturespace.org.nz

Making seed bombs
www.maararoa.org.nz

Epiphyte survey
www.nzepiphytenetwork.org

NICOLA TOKI

TV: Meet the Locals
www.doc.govt.nz/get-involved/conservation-
activities/meet-the-locals-videos/all-meet
-the-locals-videos

Radio: RNZ Critter of the Week
www.radionz.co.nz/national/programmes/
afternoons/collections/critter-of-the-week

Books written under the name
Nicola Vallance:

Nic's New Zealand Nature: Invaders,
New Holland, 2009

Nic's New Zealand Nature: Wild Buddies
and Baddies, New Holland, 2012

Threatened species ambassador
www.doc.govt.nz

Which lizards are found in different regions
www.doc.govt.nz/nature/native-animals

Attracting lizards to your garden
www.doc.govt.nz/get-involved

New Zealand Herpetological Society
www.reptiles.org.nz

ANTHONY BEHRENS

The Palmy Pine Pulling Posse
www.youtube.com/watch?v=cCqo68tQCfU

Te Araroa: New Zealand's Trail
www.teararoa.org.nz

Blogsite about Te Araroa and Spine of the Fish journeys
www.whiowhio.nz/blog.html

Local weed-busting groups
www.naturespace.org.nz

Weed ID and weed-busting tips
www.weedbusters.org.nz

Plant Me Instead booklets for each region.

National Pest Plant Accord list
www.inaturalist.nz/home

Weed Control Guide
www.bionet.nz/assets

Weed-busting tips
qeiinationaltrust.org.nz

Use your local council website for weed advice

Wilding conifers
www.wildingconifers.org.nz

JORDAN ARIA HOUSIAUX

Information about sharks
www.doc.govt.nz
www.whitesharkconservationtrust.org.nz
www.fisheries.govt.nz

Beach clean-up
www.loveyourcoast.org.nz
www.sustainablecoastlines.org
www.litterintelligence.org
hotspot.org.nz
osof.org/portfolio/plastic-free-nz

RANGATAHI, YOUTH NATURE HEROES

Brandon Intermediate Enviro Team
About their project
mountainstoseawellington.org/cannons-creek-lake-and-kenepuru-stream
mountainstoseawellington.org/about-us

Bird of the Year
www.birdoftheyear.org.nz

Youth Ambassadors
www.visitzealandia.com
Or contact your local zoo, wildlife reserve or sanctuary to check for youth ambassador roles.

Young Birders NZ
www.youngbirdersnz.com

George Hobson interview
www.radionz.co.nz/national/programmes/afternoons/audio/2018650800/youth-award-for-teen-conservationist

www.radionz.co.nz/national/programmes/ourchangingworld/audio/2018666023/banding-together-for-banded-dotterels

Riley Hathaway
Riley and Steve's TEDx Talk
www.youtube.com/watch?v=UzA_CTkn7vk

Young Ocean Explorers: Love our Ocean, Riley and Steve Hathaway, available from youngoceanexplorers.myshopify.com

Young Ocean Explorers
www.youngoceanexplorers.com

Speaking up for nature
'Psychology for a Better World: working with people to save the planet' address by Niki Harre
www.youtube.com/watch?v=2zExibEV_PY

Writing persuasive letters
vln.school.nz/groupcms/view/845343/persuasive-writing

Keeping safe online
www.netsafe.org.nz/staying-safe-online

PHOTOGRAPHIC CREDITS

6. Pōhutukawa, Rob Lucas

8–9. On the watch, c.1900. Dr Roberts photograph, Hocken Collections Uare Taokao Hākena, University of Otago, P1966-004-001a.

9. Mr R. Henry's residence, Pigeon Island, c.1900. Photographer unknown, Hocken Collections Uare Taoka o Hākena, University of Otago, P1966-004-002.

9. Lassie ready for work, c.1900. Hocken Collections Uare Taokao Hākena, University of Otago, P1966-004-005.

9. Kiwi, c.1900. Hocken Collections Uare Taokao Hākena, University of Otago, P1978-017-001.

9. Map of Dusky Sound, Land Information New Zealand (LINZ)

10. Kākāpo, Jake Osborne

10. Stoat & trap, Rod Morris www.rodmorris.co.nz

11. DOC worker, Jake Osborne

11. Anchor Island, Dusky Sound, Craig Potton

12. Chew card, Otago Peninsula Biodiversity Group

12. Tracking tunnel, DOC

15. Coquille Bay, Shutterstock

15. Elsie Farrelly in Girl Guide uniform, PAColl-7842-1-21-2, Alexander Turnbull Library

15. Diary illustration, Floor van Lierop

16. *Piwakawaka*, Pérrine Moncrieff, Alexander Turnbull Library, A-001-043-1

17. Book signing, Nelson Provincial Museum GCW 2708 Frame 7

19. Bird-watching, Forest & Bird

20. Lance Richdale with royal albatross chick, Richdale Archive, Hocken Collections | Uare Taoka o Hākena

21. Lance Richdale with royal albatross chick, Terry O'Callaghan collection

21. Royal albatross chick, Richdale Archive, Hocken Collections | Uare Taoka o Hākena

21. Taiaroa Head, Shutterstock

22. Royal albatross flying, Shutterstock

22. Royal albatross with chick, Richdale Archive, Hocken Collections | Uare Taoka o Hākena

23. Little penguin and yellow-eyed penguin, Rod Morris www.rodmorris.co.nz

23. Sparrow being banded, New Zealand National Bird Banding Scheme/DOC

25. Little penguin in a box, Kerry-Jayne Wilson

25. Little penguin, Zoë Breukel

26. Betty Batham with Hubert Ryburn, Special Collections, University of Otago

27. Betty Batham's illustrations from card database: www.marineinfo. otago.ac.nz/web/marineinfo.php

27. RV *Munida*, Otago University, Department of Marine Science records, MS-3302/357, S14-512a

30. Don Merton (top), Rod Morris www.rodmorris.co.nz

30. Don Merton, Errol Nye/DOC

31. Saddlebacks, Shutterstock

32. Tūī, Stan Sutton

33. Black robin, Rod Morris www.rodmorris.co.nz

33. Silvereyes, Steve Attwood

34–36. George Gibbs

36. Wētāpunga, Rod Morris www.rodmorris.co.nz

36. Raukumara wētā, George Gibbs

37. Wētā motel, Gillian Candler

38. Ingrid Visser, Juan Coppello

39. Ingrid Visser, R. van Meurs

39. Newspaper clipping, *Northern Advocate*

40. Ingrid Visser, Terry Hardie

42, 44. Miriam Ritchie

43. Beau, Andrew Glaser Neo, DOC

46–48. Pātaka Moore and Caleb Royal, Pātaka Moore

46. Mangapouri Stream, Adrian Heke/ Ministry of Education

47. Children at the river, Melanie McColgan

48. Painting drains, Enviroschools Nelson

49. Schools looking after streams, Melanie McColgan

50–53. Catherine Kirby, Steve Pearce

51. Puka root, Catherine Kirby

54. Nicola Toki, Quinn Berenston

55. Tuatara with wētā, Rod Morris www.rodmorris.co.nz

57. Lizard garden, Gillian Candler

57. Elegant gecko, Rod Morris www.rodmorris.co.nz

58–60. Anthony Behrens and Fiona, Anthony Behrens

58. Fernbird, David Hallet

59. Whio, Andy Trowbridge

62. Jordan Aria Housiaux

63. Shark, Shutterstock

64–65. Beach clean-up, Joe Dowling

65. Dead gannet, Shutterstock

66. Brandon Intermediate School, Mountains to Sea, Wellington

67. George Hobson, Nikki McArthur

67. Banded dotterel, George Hobson

68–69. Riley and Steve Hathaway, Armie Armstrong

69–71. Mountains to Sea, Wellington

All illustrations and uncredited photos throughout: Floor van Lierop

The publishers have attempted to gain permission/copyright clearance for all photographs used in this book, If, however, you are the copyright holder of a photograph for which clearance has not been obtained, please contact the publishers and we shall attempt to remedy the situation.

ABOUT THE AUTHOR

Gillian Candler is an award-winning author who brings her knowledge and skills in education and publishing to her passion for the natural world. The more she learns about the extraordinary wildlife of Aotearoa, the more inspired she is to help protect our native species.

When she's not writing books, Gillian volunteers on conservation projects, such as counting birds, monitoring lizards, trapping pests, advocating for little penguins, making seed balls, and helping with bird and lizard translocations. Gillian lives on the coast in Pukerua Bay.

ACKNOWLEDGEMENTS

The author gratefully acknowledges the support of the CLNZ Contestable Fund.

Many thanks to all the nature heroes featured in the book. You are an inspiration to us all. Particular thanks to George Gibbs, Ingrid Visser, Miriam Ritchie, Pātaka Moore, Caleb Royal, Catherine Kirby, Nicola Toki, Anthony Behrens, Jordan Aria Housiaux, Marley Fretton, Mayala Parau, Jak Ruatapu, Ezra Crawshaw, George Hobson and Riley Hathaway who all generously gave their time to tell me about their work.

Thanks, too, to Rebecca McCormack, Colin Miskelly, Sally Carson of NZ Marine Studies Centre, Sally Thomas and Pete Barton at Department of Conservation, Richard Wesley

from Leave No Trace, Jacqui Watts-Pointer at Brandon Intermediate School, Zoe Studd from Mountains to Sea Wellington, all of whom read sections of the book and gave feedback. Also thanks to Keith Probert and John Jillett who shared memories of Betty Batham.

Among the many organisations who helpfully answered questions were: Pest Detective, Garden Bird Survey, Birds NZ Wader Counts, NZ Marine Studies Centre, Orca Research Trust, Department of Conservation, Leave No Trace, Weedbusters, Mountains to Sea Wellington, Porirua Harbour Trust, Brandon Intermediate School. Many others answered questions or shared ideas about which heroes to include. Thank you all for your interest in the project; you are too numerous to name.

Many of the ideas in this book were inspired by projects I've been involved in. I'd like to acknowledge all the volunteers I've worked with at Friends of Maara Roa, Friends of Mana Island, Kāpiti Biodiversity Project, Ngā Uruora, Predator Free Pukerua Bay, Zealandia, Forest & Bird, Birds New Zealand. The wētā motel pictured on page 37 was made by the MenzShed Kāpiti.

Finally, I would like to acknowledge editor Jude Watson, the team at Potton & Burton, and in particular Floor van Lierop's design for *Nature Heroes*, which has well and truly brought this book to life.

First published in 2019 by
Potton & Burton
319 Hardy Street,
PO Box 221 Nelson
New Zealand
pottonandburton.co.nz

© Gillian Candler

Design & illustrations:
Floor van Lierop
thisisthem.com

ISBN 978 1 98 8550 01 5

Printed in China by Everbest